THE MASSACRE AT ATÅTE

JOSE M. TORRES

The Massacre at Atåte

Jose M. Torres

Copyright © 2021, 2016, 2014 by Jose M. Torres.
All rights reserved.

Copyright is meant to respect the imagination, artistry, research and hard work that go into bringing a book to life. Please respect all copyright laws by not reproducing this book in any manner without permission from the publisher except in brief quotations used for research, private studies, critical texts or reviews.

Published by MARC Publications, University of Guam Press
Richard F. Taitano Micronesian Area Research Center (MARC)
303 University Drive, UOG Station
Mangilao, Guam 96923
(671) 735-2154

www.uogpress.com

Second Edition, 2021
ISBN 978-1-935198-62-8
Library of Congress Control Number: 2021945424

Second Edition Copy Edits by Victoria-Lola Leon Guerrero and Via De Fant
Chamorro edits by Joey Franquez
Second Edition Cover Design and Layout by Ralph Eurich Patacsil
Historical Notes and Timeline by Michael Lujan Bevacqua, Ph.D.
Book Indexing by Elizabeth Kelley Bowman, Ph.D. and Ralph Eurich Patacsil
Front Cover Illustration "I Mammatatnga giya Malesso'" by Jack Lujan Bevacqua
Inside Cover "Atåte Map" from the MARC Collections
Back Cover Photo from Jose M. Torres

The first edition of this publication was made possible by a grant from the Guam Preservation Trust.

Note: The author chose to follow an older orthography in his spelling of the word Chamorro. The word is now spelled "CHamoru" according to the official Guam orthography.

Historical notes and important dates have been added throughout the book to provide greater context about the passage of time during the war and about significant moments and events in Guam's history.

This book is dedicated to the forty-six *Tinta* and *Fåha* victims, who underwent insufferable fear and mental anguish before the craven enemy snuffed out their lives for no other reason than they, the savages and cowards that they were, could do so.

CONTENTS

Introduction | **1**

The Last Feast | **9**

Prewar Years (Historical Notes) | **15**

Pre-war Malesso' | **18**

A Sign of the Changing Times | **28**

The Path to War and Invasion of Guam (Historical Notes) | **31**

The Japanese Occupation of Malesso' | **36**

Occupation (Historical Notes) | **45**

Laboring from Dusk to Dawn | **48**

My Search for Atåte | **61**

I Found My People | **65**

The Tinta Massacre | **67**

Final Tragedies and Trauma (Historical Notes) | **71**

The Massacre of the Japanese at Atåte | **74**

The Japanese Are Choked to Death | **78**

Six Volunteers to Contact the Americans Stepped Up | **80**

An Additional Dead Japanese | **81**

In Search of Help from the Americans | **82**

Guam's liberation begins in Atåte (Historical Notes) | **87**

On the Open Seas in Search of Help | **92**

Put Ashore | **99**

My People Arrive at the Hågat Camp | **101**

The Malesso' People Return Home | **102**

We Reach Our Låncho | **104**

The Fåha Victims Found | **105**

A Tribute to Jose "Pop Tonko" Soriano Reyes | **106**

Afterword | **112**

Appendices | **154**

ACKNOWLEDGEMENTS

The author acknowledges with deep and lasting thanks and appreciation University of Guam professors Michael Lujan Bevacqua (Chamorro Studies), Anne Perez Hattori (History/Chamorro Studies) and Elizabeth Kelley Bowman (Literature/Women and Gender Studies) as well as UOG students Derick Bascon, Blaine C. Dydasco, Julie Jasmin, Elyssa Santos and Anthony Tornito for their generous, unselfish and lasting contributions to this work. I also wish to acknowledge the artistic help of Jack Lujan Bevacqua, who created the image for the cover and Robert Tenorio, who photographed the Tinta and Fåha massacre sites. Finally, I want to thank my friend Todd Thompson for his support and for encouraging me, like many of my other friends did, to commit my memories to paper after all these years.

Jose M. Torres
October 24, 2014

INTRODUCTION

"Puno' i Et Diablo: Killing the Devil in Malesso'"

Robert Anacletus Underwood
*University of Guam President Emeritus
and Former Member of Congress*

This first-hand account of the massacre of Japanese soldiers at Atåte performs many tasks for those interested in the history of the Chamorro people and their experiences during World War II. It is at once a first-hand account of a historical experience and history itself. Jose "Peling" Torres has granted his people and the rest of us an inspiring and sobering story about human strength and frailty in the midst of struggle and hardship.

But it is more than the usual World War II story of Chamorro suffering and endurance usually placed into the larger and overwhelming tapestry of Japanese cruelty and American military strength. It is about Chamorro action. It is about Chamorro strength. It is about overt resistance and the leadership of Tonko Reyes. In

The *kampanåyon* or belltower, one of the most enduring landmarks of the village of Malesso'.

*From the Collections of the Division of the Guam Museum,
a division of the Department of Chamorro Affairs*

historical narratives, we usually have heroes and villains. We also have victims. For the World War II experience, Chamorros have usually been just victims, responding but rarely acting; moaning in agony, being slapped, working like slaves, but rarely moving in the opposite direction.

In Malesso', some young men, mostly in their teens, decided to take action. Their village compatriots and relatives were massacred by the dozens at Faha' and Tinta. Under the leadership of Pop Tonko' Reyes, they conspired to attack the Japanese soldiers who were known to them. These soldiers were assigned to Malesso'. Without training, they carried out their conspiracy and killed several Japanese soldiers.

When teenagers who didn't go as far as the fifth or sixth grade in school decide to take matters into their own hands, we expect a valiant, but unsuccessful outcome. This was not the case. They carried out their conspiracy with their own hands and fled to neighboring American war ships on outrigger canoes. It was perhaps the greatest testimony to native-born instincts in Guam during the 20th century. Trained only in the hills and waters of Malesso', fed by the outrage of the massacres and inspired by their own sense of right and wrong, they took action.

In the scheme of things, this particular account did little to affect the war, but it will contribute enormously to the redefinition of the war experience and the "agency" of the Chamorro people. Jose Torres's account will be read, reread and assigned reading for school children for the next two generations. It is both history and literature. It will dwarf in significance other first-hand accounts and I am sure that there will be challenges to it from descendants of family members who were told a different account.

Sometimes people misunderstand first-hand information as "history." History is the written account of an event in narrative form.

These days we have additional avenues from DVDs and films to help bring out the historical narrative in audio-visual account and social media. However, first-hand information, while useful in creating a historical narrative, is clearly not the same thing as history itself. Instead, first-hand information is the raw material for narratives and must be analyzed for accuracy, relevance and significance. There is some raw material in Jose Torres's account, but fortunately for us, there is lots of history.

It is also literature in that it is filled with compelling human details and dramas. Witness the two women who had two very different responses about the killing of the Japanese soldiers. Read about the Chamorro "faker" who fooled the Japanese into beating up one of his enemies and later, into letting him go back to Malesso' because he was sick. He eventually got his comeuppance in Humåtak after the Americans had landed and all seemed secure.

But it is mostly just about ordinary young people thrown into extraordinary circumstances and who decided to do something about it. Would teenagers from any other generation do the same thing? Who will be that group for the 21st century? It may not require plotting an attack on soldiers, but it could necessitate similar levels of courage and determination.

Despite their enthusiasm, they still needed a plan and a spark.. That spark of leadership came from Pop Reyes. He wasn't that much older. What a man! What a hero! What a CHamoru!

Si Yu'os ma'ase' Siñot Torres put i tinige'-mu. Ha pacha i korason-ta yan ha ekstende mit beses yan mas i kinemprende-ta put i tiempon gera.

Photo of Robert A. Underwood is courtesy of the Office of the President, University of Guam

The Massacre at Atåte

Jose M. Torres

THE LAST FEAST

Monday, December 8, 1941 was the Feast of the Immaculate Conception, a church holiday. After Mass, we all went home for breakfast and later returned to the church grounds for a volleyball game. While we were setting up the volleyball net, we heard loud explosions coming from the northwest. We all thought it was the activity of defense contractors now working around the clock to fortify the island. The project had been approved by the U.S. Congress following a lengthy debate on whether Guam needed to be militarily fortified against the Japanese, who were belligerently talking about a war against the United States.

    Less than an hour later, there was this car careening into town, its horn blaring: "Sumay has been bombed by the Japanese!" the passengers shouted. The attackers were identified as Japanese from the markings on the planes' wings and fuselages. Many of the islanders had also learned of the Japanese attack on Pearl Harbor through the short-wave radio news.

    I immediately took off for home. When I got there, my mother had already rounded up my siblings and we all ran to a relative's *låncho* in the *Geus* river valley. There we joined two other families and we all fled into the jungle at *Langan* at the eastern wall of *Geus* valley. There, it was thought that the thick foliage would effectively hide us from marauding Japanese war planes. Our elders believed that the

A common feature of daily life in prewar Malesso' was the roof-thatching party. Family and friends would gather together and help weave and thatch a neighbor's roof.

From the Collections of the Division of the Guam Museum, a division of the Department of Chamorro Affairs

enemy would spot us unless we were hidden by the dense foliage. Later that day, as we were hiding in the jungle, an enemy warplane flew overhead and dropped a bomb. But if the pilot had targeted a building in the American barracks complex in the western end of the village, his aim was way off. The bomb created an unimpressively shallow crater hundreds of feet from the nearest building.

Way before dawn the next day, we again went into the jungle where we remained for the entire day. We moved back into the *Geus låncho* only after dark. And since the prior days were uneventful – no bombing threats by the Japanese – it was decided that we need not return to the jungle the next day.

Early Wednesday morning, December 10, the womenfolk started preparing a breakfast of *kadun månnok*. It would be the first substantive and full meal we would have eaten since the preceding Monday. Just before we started eating, there was a cry of alarm by some of our people. There was this smallish man, dressed in khaki, wearing toeless canvas shoes, a band of khaki cloth winding up his lower legs and cloth flaps from his cap covering his ears. He was also carrying a rifle and peering into the clump of bamboo where the womenfolk had fled after the alarm had been sounded. The strange man was a Japanese soldier. We later learned that he was part of the contingent which had landed by sea early that morning in Malesso'.

One of the three *padres de familia* with us now stepped forward. The patriarch had previously worked at a Japanese store in downtown Hagåtña and could speak some Japanese. He started to talk to the visitor. He then took a bowl and filled it with soup and practically all of the chicken pieces that had been prepared. With a plate of rice, he handed the food to the Japanese, who hungrily devoured it with much belching and farting. After he was sated, he walked away without saying a word.

That incident was my introduction to the Japanese who, for two and a half years, brutally occupied the island of my birth. In the end, however, half a score of these armed enemies were themselves massacred in a place called Atåte by wrathful, brazen, brave, and emboldened compatriots of my village. The account of that massacre, published for the first time by someone who was there, is the central purpose of this story.

HISTORICAL NOTES

PREWAR YEARS

Guam was taken by the United States in 1898, after more than 200 years of Spanish rule. Whereas the Spanish empire was coming to an end in the 19th century, the U.S. was rising in power and gaining influence. Guam's value to the U.S. was as a strategic colony, operating as a port that could help U.S. ships get across the Pacific to Asia. The U.S. Navy was given control over Guam and the lives of the Chamorro people. Whoever was the commander of the U.S. Navy base on Guam was also the governor of the island.

The U.S. brought new opportunities into the island during the years prior to World War II. Education was made available to all young children. The U.S. Navy employed more Chamorros, especially as teachers. Modern infrastructure expanded on the island with the construction of more roads, power plants and eventually telephone lines. Chamorros began to listen to and watch American media that came in through movie theaters and over the radio.

Despite these developments, Guam was still a colony or possession of the U.S. and was not a full and equal part of the country or an independent country of its own. Guam was segregated under the U.S. in terms of schools and wages. Health care was provided with the taxes collected from Chamorros. Even though schools were open to all, the Chamorro language was banned and the curriculum had no connection to the daily lives of the Chamorro people.

During this period, Chamorros worked to make the best of new opportunities, but regularly petitioned for more political rights, a local government and U.S. citizenship.

1936 B.J. Bordallo and F.B. Leon Guerrero travel to Washington D.C. to lobby the U.S. government for more political rights for the Chamorro people. Despite meeting with many leaders, including President Franklin Delano Roosevelt, they are not successful.

1937 Dr. Ramon Manalisay Sablan, the first Chamorro doctor, returns to Guam after attending college in the U.S. to set up his own medical practice.

1938 The first local educational board is established on Guam, but due to the general lack of self-governance under the U.S. Navy, it is only an advisory board.

1938 The Hepburn Report recommends that Guam be fortified in anticipation of possible war with Japan. American leaders ignore this recommendation as other strategic analysis has determined that Guam cannot be effectively defended against invasion.

1940 The Guam census shows a population of 23,067, with the majority of residents living in Hagåtña.

November 3, 1940 A terrifying typhoon hits the island, destroying most homes and killing most livestock.

February 14, 1941 President Franklin Delano Roosevelt signs Executive Order 8683, which requires anyone entering or leaving Guam to have a security clearance from the U.S. Navy. This is kept in effect until 1962.

April 5, 1941 Påle' Oscar Lujan Calvo, the 3rd ever Chamorro-Catholic priest, is ordained in Guam.

1941 *Guam and its People* is published by anthropologist Dr. Laura Thompson. She did most of her fieldwork for the book on Guam from 1938-1939 while living in Malesso'.

PRE-WAR MALESSO'

Malesso' (Merizo to many other people) is the southernmost community on the island. Pre-war, the village was nearly a mile long and few people lived beyond its eastern and western borders. The eastern border of the village was made up of the fertile farmlands that our people had cultivated for many, many years. Immediately to the east of the village was the *Geus* River Valley. For generations, it was the main rice-growing area for the people. Further out were farmlands on which people raised other Chamorro staples: taro, bananas, corn, tapioca, sweet potatoes, yams. Dotting the broad expanse of the Malesso' farmlands stood the breadfruit trees whose seasonal fruits were (and still are) much loved by the people. Before the war, farmers typically slept in the village at night. At daybreak, they would walk or ride a *karabao* or a *karabao* bullcart to their farms. The *karabao* was the beast of burden and hardly any family in Malesso' was without one. This work routine was observed daily, except on Sunday, which was a day of rest.

Malesso' was well circumscribed, with farms and water creating its natural borders. The village is fronted by *Dåno'*[1] and the broad *Dåno'* lagoon. The *Mamaon* Channel, a deep-water channel, runs adjacent to the shallow waters by the village. The channel extends

---

1   Cocos Island

A typical scene in prewar Malesso'.*

A Chamorro fisherman mending his nets.*

*From the Collections of the Division of the Guam Museum,
a division of the Department of Chamorro Affairs*

for nearly a mile from the open ocean to the west and ends in a *cul-de-sac* at the channel's eastern end. *Dåno'*, its lagoon and the *Mamaon* Channel have provided food for the sustenance of our people since historic times. Offshore, *Dåno'* lagoon teemed with fish that were easily caught by all sorts of fishing methods. Occasionally, there would be runs of mackerel and *mañåhak*[2] that were fried, salted or pickled in brine and served as local delicacies. Mackerel runs occurred from time to time in the *Mamaon* Channel. The fish, in a large school, would enter the channel from open and deeper waters to the west and travel to spawn at the channel's eastern end. There, the fish (most of which weighed about a pound each) would be netted and later scooped onto boats or onto dry land.

Directing the entire fishing operation would be Antonio Leon Guerrero Cruz, also known as *Tun Antonion Ana* (We will meet this amazing gentleman further on in our story). After the fish were netted, *Tun Antonio* would then determine the size of the catch and its apportionment to the people who helped make the entire catch. The largest share of the catch would go to the divers (the ones with face masks or goggles) who cast the net around the school as it came in and later checked that there was no breach in the bottom of the net from which fish could escape. The next largest share would go to the net owner, followed by the owners of the boats used in the process, then to those who handled part of the net and finally to the bystanders who had come by merely to ogle at the activities. *Tun Antonio* had maintained that the mackerel was God's bounty and that everyone should share a portion of the catch.

Mañåhak runs occur more frequently around the earlier part of the year. Each of the fish measures about an inch or slightly more. When thousands of them are in schools, these runs are easily spotted

---

2   Juvenile rabbitfish

Two young boys posing with a *galaide'* on the beach in Malesso'.

*From the Collections of the Division of the Guam Museum,
a division of the Department of Chamorro Affairs*

as brownish, slowly moving masses. Most *mañåhak* netting teams consist of three or more people: two people hold the net while one or more drive the fish toward the net by splashing the water and making noise. Some fishermen also use fine mesh throw nets to catch *mañåhak*. In anticipation of these runs, most every family in the village would prepare by making salt to preserve the fish as *inasnin mañåhak*[3], a delicacy for most Chamorros.

Malesso' was a sedate village where everyone knew everyone else. In December 1941, the village's population was approximately 866 people, only four of whom were non-Chamorros: the American Capuchin priest, Father Marcian Pellet, pastor of the village's San Dimas Church; a Filipina, Maria Lukban Mesa, the principal of the village's public school who was married to Tomas Mesa, a dental student in Manila at the time the war started; a Marine sergeant assigned to the village as a law-enforcement officer; and a U.S. Navy corpsman who ran the village's dispensary/medical clinic.

Events of great importance, like the celebration of the feast day of the village's patron saint, San Dimas, the "good thief," were observed by the whole village. The fiesta was an immovable feast. If the day, April 24, fell on a weekday, why, the fiesta would be celebrated on that week day. A religious procession, which wound through the village, was held on the eve of the saint's feast day. Following the procession, *ná taotao tumano*, literally "food for those who walked," was served. Devotees of San Dimas, some of whom lived in Hagåtña, Inalåhan, Talo'fo'fo, and other distant places had made a sacred *promessa* to walk to Malesso' to attend the procession and Mass honoring their patron saint. It was for these pilgrims that the host-villagers chose and prepared food to serve. The following day after the festal Mass, visitors were welcomed in every household to share food that

---

3   Salted *mañåhak*.

was traditionally loved by the Chamorro people.

Weddings in Malesso' were also important celebratory events, not only for the principals (the bride and the groom) but for almost everyone in the village. After the two sets of parents agreed to a marriage (the prospective principals hardly had any say in most of the wedding plans and their execution), wedding banns would be announced at three consecutive Sunday Masses. The wedding would then take place on Saturday after the final bann had been announced.

In Chamorro society, the groom's family provided the dowry: wedding dress, wedding ring and other jewelry; every-day apparel for the bride; and in some instances the livestock (poultry, pigs, cattle) that would be consumed during the festivities. Unlike in some other societies, money dowries were not provided by the groom's family. About three weeks before the wedding, the groom's family arranged for the bride-to-be to be's wedding dress fitting. The dress would most often be sewn by a local seamstress. A chest was later bought to contain the wedding dress, a few ordinary dresses, the wedding band, gold rings, bracelets and other fine jewelry. The presentation of the dowry chest to the bride's family was done with little ceremony, but later, the bride's neighbors, her relatives and others would all come to her residence to ogle at the dowry contained in the chest.

The wedding highlight is the *komplimento*, which took place on the eve of the wedding. Tradition was that the groom's group would organize an entourage that would then travel afoot to the bride's place. At around six in the evening, the entourage, consisting of the groom, his parents, siblings, godparents, close relatives, virtually every other villager and a string band would all begin to assemble. Around seven o'clock, the band would start to play and walk to the bride's place.

The entourage would be welcomed by a greeter who would then formally invite the group into the house for a period of merriment

Three men of Malesso' weaving coconut leaves to be used for roof thatching.

From the Collections of the Division of the Guam Museum, a division of the Department of Chamorro Affairs

that included dancing, singing, eating and drinking. *Tuba*, the fermented and intoxicating form of the coconut sap, was passed all around. *Aguayiente*, the inebriating distillate from fermented *tuba*, was also consumed in copious quantity. The liquor may have been produced without a license from the authorities and so the spirit consumed at the wedding party could very well have been moonshine. But what law-enforcement official would have the courage and temerity to officially confront the law-breaker(s) when everyone else was partying and having a good time? A most inopportune time for such confrontation to occur, I'd say!

After a period of merriment, it was time for the main event of the evening: the dance by the soon-to-be-wedded couple. In the bride's living room, the revelers would form a ring in the center of which the couple dances, most often to the tune of a *båtso*, or waltz, by the band with the party-goers ogling, applauding, stomping and egging them on. After the dance, the *nobia* and *nobiu* would retire to their respective homes to get some rest for the nuptial Mass the next morning. The wedding took place at the village church's 6 a.m. Mass. The bride's family would sponsor the post-wedding breakfast, a sedate event in comparison to the sometimes wild merry-making the night before at the bride's home.

Daily life combined work with community interaction. One of the many happy moments of my teen-aged life occurred when I got to join our neighbors, *Tun Miget* and *Tan Trudis*, on one of their frequent trips to *Dåno'* to gather resources for daily living. Due to a dynamite accident, *Tun Miget* had lost his right eye as well as three fingers on his right hand. But those losses didn't deter him from continuing to diligently work his farm and fish the ocean to sustain his family. He was also a superb sailor who could expertly tack his outrigger canoe with its lateen sail to *Dåno'* and back to the mainland.

Like they say, half the fun was sailing to *Dåno'* from the mainland.

Dåno' abounds in large coconut crabs, *ayuyu*, which are best hunted at night. But if one cuts open a few ripe coconuts and place them in the open, the crustaceans would then come out to feed on the coconut meat and the trapper would have no problem gathering them up.

Our chores were all cut out for each of us upon reaching the island. Soon after we touched land, *Tun Miget* would take off with his throw net to catch fish for lunch. After a short while, he would return with still-thrashing, freshly caught fish which *Tan Trudis* would promptly prepare for roasting over open fire. Our lunch would be *tininun guihan* with the *titayas mai'es Tan Trudis* would bring over. *Tan Trudis* would cook lunch for us and weave coconut frond baskets to contain some of the stuff we gathered. *Tan Trudis* would also pick *atkaparas*[4] which, when pickled, was a gourmet item for us.

One of my chores was to produce salt. A large caldron was permanently installed for use by anyone wanting to make salt from the crystalline waters surrounding the island. One would fill the caldron with salt water, light a fire of ironwood logs under the big pot and monitor the process to make sure that there was always enough salt-water in the caldron and adequate fire underneath to keep the salt-water boiling. When the salt-maker decided that enough salt had been produced, the remaining fluid would be boiled off and what was left was a thick layer of crystalline salt.

My other job was to make charcoal for the flat-iron back home. Ironwood charcoal was best because it burned longer and hotter. The process of making charcoal involved burning large ironwood logs and then dousing the fire after the charcoal had been adequately produced.

When the sun started to dip earnestly to the western horizon, we would return to the mainland. The canoe would be laden with

---

4   Capers

what we had gathered for the day: firewood, charcoal, salt, salted fish, *atkaparas*, *ayuyu* and large land crabs. With the northeast winds blowing earnestly toward *Dåno'* (and against our craft), *Tun Miget* would skillfully tack and soon we'd arrive at our home beach tired but happy that we had brought home some of what we needed for our daily living.

A SIGN OF THE CHANGING TIMES

Malesso' was an agricultural village and, for the longest time, the principal cash crop was *copra*, the dried meat of the coconut. We sustained ourselves with the food we got from the land and sea, but money was needed to buy other things, such as clothes, building materials and even some food items like coffee, rice, sugar and flour for the *titiyas arina* and *buñelos* that virtually every Chamorro loved. There were but a few paying jobs available. Except for the school teachers (and there were awfully few of them), there were few people earning money, and thus money was scarce.

In the early 1930s, this changed. Tomas Espinosa Cruz or *Tun Tomas Domma*, a village general merchandise store owner, bought a flat-bed truck not only to transport merchandise from downtown Hagåtña to his Malesso' store but also to haul fresh fruits and vegetables, grown in Malesso', to the farmers' market that operated in the capital city every Saturday morning. Truck farming suddenly became profitable and Malesso' farmers started raising cabbages, eggplants, string beans, cantaloupes, watermelons and other fruits and vegetables for commercial sale.

I remember the mango tree in our backyard. Every year it produced a lot of fruit, which, when ripe, we ate with much relish. But one can only eat so many ripe mangos and after a while, the tree-ripened fruits simply fell to the ground and nobody bothered to pick them up. But with the advent of *Tun Tomas* and his truck hauling fresh fruits and vegetables to the Hagåtña market, we started to pick the fruit off the tree before they were really ripe. They were then stored in a dark, warm place (usually under a bed) where they would ripen to be included in *Tun Tomas's* haul to the market where the fragrant, sweet and succulent mangos always fetched a good price.

HISTORICAL NOTES

THE PATH TO WAR AND THE INVASION OF GUAM

World War II began in Asia in the 1930s, with the Japanese seeking to expand their territories in Manchuria and China. By 1939, war had also broken out in Europe. News of the war regularly reached Guam, especially as relations between the U.S. and Japan grew more tense. The U.S. government and military was divided in their opinion over what to do with Guam, even as the Japanese gained new territories in Micronesia and began to build up its military in those islands.

U.S. military strategists didn't think Guam could be defended from a Japanese attack, and so decisions were made not to prepare the island. Historian Don Farrell refers to this as "the sacrifice" of Guam, where rather than expend money or effort to protect Guam, the U.S. decided to let it be taken, thinking it would be easier and cheaper to take it back later. The impact on and interests of the Chamorro people were not considered in these decisions.

As the U.S. and Japan moved closer to potential war in 1941, money was set aside to improve Guam militarily, anticipating a Japanese attack. On island, the U.S. Navy prepared itself for war, but did not prepare the Chamorro population. In October 1941, Navy dependents on Guam were evacuated to the U.S. for safety. When Chamorros serving in the U.S. Navy tried to have their families evacuated, they were told that only white people would be evacuated. White men with Chamorro or Filipina wives were told that their wives could not be evacuated.

In December 1941, the U.S. knew that a Japanese attack was imminent, and the Naval Governor of Guam was ordered to destroy all classified and secret files. The U.S. Navy publicly proclaimed that the people did not have to worry, because the Japanese would never dare to attack America. Privately, Navy officers who were close to Chamorro families told them to hide food and prepare for war.

When Japanese planes flew overhead on the morning of December 8, 1941, a majority of Guam's Chamorro people were participating in Catholic mass services for the Feast of the Immaculate Conception instead of preparing for the coming war and occupation.

A few hours after the Japanese attack at Pearl Harbor, Japanese bombers from other islands in Micronesia bombed Guam on December 8, 1941. Their first targets were focused in Sumay, the second most populous village on the island.

The lack of war preparation from the U.S. was obvious as soon as the first bombs from the Japanese hit their targets in Sumay. The U.S. military presence on the island was less than 500 men, few of whom had ever seen a real battle.

On December 10, 1941 when the Japanese invaded the island, they did so with more than 5,500 men, most of whom had been battle tested in wars on the Asian continent. The American defense of the island didn't last very long, although some Chamorros, especially in the last stand at the Plaza de España in Hagåtña, fought with great courage.

After the first bombs were dropped, most families fled Hagåtña and other villages, escaping to farms or the jungle. After the fighting ended on December 10th, all island residents were called out to register their families. The initial shock of the occupation was reinforced as many Chamorros were slapped by Japanese soldiers for not bowing to them or showing sufficient respect.

All American civilians and military personnel were rounded up and kept prisoner in the Cathedral in Hagåtña. There were rumors that America would return promptly to retake the island and rescue the American officers and civilians held captive. These rumors soon proved false when in January, all Americans and other foreign nationals were taken by ship to prisoner of war camps in Japan.

September 18, 1931 Japanese forces invade Manchuria, which is the first in a series of aggressive Japanese actions that precipitate World War II.

September 1, 1939 German forces invade Poland sparking World War II in Europe.

February – March 1941 The U.S. Congress, worried about possible war with Japan, appropriates more than $4 million for last-minute defensive improvements in Guam.

April 1941 The Guam Militia, which had been disbanded by the U.S. Navy in 1938, is reorganized as the Insular Force Guard.

July 26, 1941 President Roosevelt orders the seizure of all Japanese assets in the United States in response to Japanese aggression against European colonies in Asia.

October 1941 A total of 104 American military and civilian dependents are evacuated from Guam to Hawaii and the West Coast of the United States. Despite pleas from several Chamorros in the U.S. Navy, no non-white dependents are evacuated.

November 1941 Japanese special envoy Saburo Kurusu stops overnight in Guam while en-route to Washington for peace talks. He spends the night at the Pan American Hotel at Sumay, which would be bombed by the Japanese a month later.

November 29, 1941 6,000 Japanese troops massing in the Bonin Islands of Japan receive orders to attack and seize Guam.

December 4, 1941 Naval Governor George McMillin receives a coded telegram that, in anticipation of a Japanese attack, he must "destroy all secret and confidential publications and other classified matter … [and] Retain minimum cryptographic channels necessary for essential communication."

December 7, 1941 Pearl Harbor in Hawai'i is attacked by Japanese forces. Seven Chamorros die while serving aboard the U.S.S. *Arizona*, which is sunk in the attack. The U.S. immediately declares war on Japan.

December 8, 1941 Japanese bombers from other islands in Micronesia bomb Guam.

December 9, 1941 Japanese planes continue to bomb and strafe strategically important targets in Hagåtña, Piti and Sumay

December 10, 1941 Early in the morning, 5,500 Japanese forces land on beaches around the island. They easily overwhelm the American defenses, and the island is surrendered by 5:45 a.m.

December 23, 1941 After initially repelling a Japanese invasion, Wake Island is surrendered. 45 Chamorros participate in its defense with 10 of them dying in the fighting.

January 6, 1942 Alfred Flores Leon Guerrero and Francisco Borja Won Pat are executed by the Japanese at Pigo cemetery.

January 10, 1942 American civilians and military personnel are placed on ships and sent to Japan to be held in prisoner of war camps.

THE JAPANESE OCCUPATION OF MALESSO'

On Wednesday, December 10, 1941, about three thousand Japanese soldiers and sailors invaded and captured the island from the Americans just two days after they initially attacked the island. In Malesso', a contingent of this group was garrisoned in buildings that were once part of the U.S. Naval radio station.

In the early 1920s, four large buildings had been built, one each for the radio facilities, barracks for the enlisted radio personnel, officer quarters and a large comfortable building for vacationing American naval officers and their families from Hagåtña. The radio complex was electrified by power lines extending over the mountains from the Hagåtña power plant. Not only was there enough electric power for the radio communications complex, but electricity was supplied to the local Catholic church, the priest's residence, the village commissioner's residence and a couple of civilian grocery stores as well. Malesso' therefore was one of only four-or-five Guam communities with electricity. The village continued to enjoy electrification until the typhoon of 1940 destroyed the power lines from Hagåtña and they were never rebuilt.

The initial sojourn in Malesso' of the Imperial Japanese Navy was short at best—about six weeks. During that time, I remember two incidents at least: one was droll, the other a harbinger of the cruelty and inhumanity we would face under Japanese rule.

Every morning a squad of soldiers would jog, in unison, from their barracks to the end of the village and back to their barracks, a distance of about four miles. Felix Espinosa San Nicolas, *Tun Felis "Akadiduk,"* a village elder (I estimate his age to have been around seventy) would wait in front of his house for the jogging soldiers and then join them. We all thought it funny to see *Tun Felis* jogging with members of the Japanese military half his age.

The other notable incident was an example of the Japanese criminal justice system (or lack of it) for the Chamorros. A group of us were forced to work cleaning the yard of one of the barracks. The *taicho*, or officer-in-charge, was supervising us. All of a sudden, a pick-up truck careened toward us, its horn blaring. When it came to a full stop, the driver got out of the car and started talking to the *taicho*, who was listening intently. Meanwhile, the two passengers in the pickup alighted from the vehicle. One of them was compressing, with a bloody piece of clothing, what appeared to be a wound on his neck. The other passenger, his face ashen and his body shaking with fear, stood rigidly at attention.

After the *taicho* had been briefed, he walked over to the fear-stricken man and hit him hard on the jaw with his right fist. The man went down but quickly stood up, took a deep bow, and again stood at attention. The *taicho* hit him again and the man was knocked down, but he quickly got up and made a deep bow. After the third blow, the man stood up again and the *taicho* waved at the driver to take him away. As they drove off, I noticed the *taicho* massaging his right fist. The alleged assailant was put in the Hagåtña jail and was there for the duration of the enemy occupation of the island.

We later learned the full story of the incident. The two men were indeed arguing, but the accused did not try to strike the neck of the other person with a machete. Our informants thought the wound was superficial and self-inflicted. A full blow by the machete would have decapitated the "victim," whom we shall meet two more times before the end of this story.

The departure from Guam of the Imperial Japanese Navy to other theaters of operation was followed by the arrival of the *Minseibu*, the entity established by the Imperial Navy for the civil administration of Guam. A contingent of the *Minseibu* was assigned to each village on island, including Malesso'.

Even before conquering Guam, the island was renamed *Omiya Jima*, literally "the island of the Imperial Court or Shinto Shrine." The island's villages were also renamed as follows:

Åsan	*Asai*
Barrigåda	*Haruta*
Dedidiu	*Hiratsuka*
Hågat	*Noka*
Hagåtña	*Akashi*
Humåtak	*Umata*
Inalåhan	*Inada*
Malesso'	*Matsuyama*
Mangilao	*Sawahara*
Piti	*Shoten*
Sinahånña	*Shinagawa*
Sumay	*Suma*
Talo'fo'fo	*Tasaki*
Yigo	*Kita*
Yo'ña	*Harakawa*

The staff of the *Minseibu*, the Japanese civilian administration of Guam during World War II.

*From the Collections of the Division of the Guam Museum,
a division of the Department of Chamorro Affairs*

Upon learning that the Japanese had renamed the island and its villages, a wiseacre was heard to remark, very discreetly of course: "*Laña*, the Japanese think they have won the war and now own the island and have started renaming our villages."

The *Minseibu* quickly issued a number of edicts, with one directing the organization of labor battalions. Soon after the Japanese conquered the island in December of 1941, they conscripted males age eleven and over into six battalions for the whole village. Members of the work battalions cultivated taro, rice, tapioca, corn and other crops without compensation because their harvests were turned over to the Japanese, who had built a warehouse with a rice mill to contain the harvested crops.

My labor battalion was Labor Battalion Number Six and had approximately thirty men and boys whose initial work was tilling and cultivating soil by hand for rice planting. The men of the labor battalions worked from sunrise to sunset, seven days a week, which gave very little time for the men to cultivate their private fields or otherwise scavenge for food in the boondocks. Some of the battalion members who owned *karabaos* and a plow would do their fieldwork well into the night after they had been dismissed from the work battalion. A popular and productive mean of fishing was the *gaddi* in which the net would be spread out and other members of the fishing group would drive the fish into the net by making noise and splashing the water. But this method of fishing was outlawed by the Japanese around 1942.

Another edict dictated everyone from ages ten to sixty to attend the weekly night school. The students were taught to recite, in Japanese, the fealty to the Japanese emperor and sing the Japanese national anthem during every school session. The school session therefore started with the *sensei* ordering the students to rise, face northwestward in the general direction of Japan, recite their allegiance to the emperor and sing the Japanese national anthem. Following this, the *sensei* would go into a tirade against the "hedonistic and morally corrupt Americans," and how the Japanese would soon win the war and, led by Prime Minister Hideki Tojo, would be dictating surrender terms to the Americans in the White House.

Among the mixed bag of students were the older ones who had toiled long and hard for their bombastic masters and only wanted for the session to end so that they could get some rest before putting in another day's labor. On the way home from one of these sessions, one of the smart-alecky younger students had composed a ditty:

Ichi, ni, san, shi, go[5]
Todu i Chapones mamba'chigo'

Normally, *ba'chigo'* had not pejorative, but on that night, it began to be. This kind of chiding resulted from the Japanese asserting themselves to the point that they behaved as though they were masters and, the natives were their serfs.

On one occasion we received another asinine edict: every family was to submit a list of livestock and poultry in its possession and may not consume any of them unless the Japanese authority gave its expressed permission. Upon receiving the edict, my uncle Vicente (one of my mother's younger brothers whom we called *Tatan Ben* because he had taken care of us since our father died in 1937) looked at his sister—my mother—and they burst out laughing. They just would not submit an accurate list and they certainly didn't intend to seek permission to have *kadun månnok* or *fritådan babui* for dinner.

And then came the edict to end all edicts: the Japanese authorities determined that houseflies had become a problem and must be

---

5   *Translation:* One, two, three, four, five All Japanese are slant-eyed.

Minseibu officials observing Chamorros as they plant rice seedlings. Most Chamorros were part of forced labor groups such as this one during World War II.

From the Collections of the Division of the Guam Museum, a division of the Department of Chamorro Affairs

eradicated. These flies were to be swatted, put in empty matchboxes and turned in to the authorities. This edict produced another guffaw from all of us—matchboxes laden with dead houseflies, indeed.

Because the menfolk were all required to work for the Japanese from sunup to sundown, there was nobody to till the soil, plant and harvest the food to sustain us. Except in rare instances when wives and other womenfolk were able to manage the plows and otherwise cultivate the soil, there were no crops to harvest. The alternative, therefore, was to forage in the jungle for edibles like wild yams, breadfruit and papayas, which was what my mother and my older sisters did while their menfolk worked for the Japanese. Even torch-hunting for land crabs and fish, a time-honored and effective night time activity for the Chamorros, was prohibited because the Japanese authorities feared that the natives were trying to signal the Americans.

HISTORICAL NOTES

OCCUPATION

In early 1942, control of Guam was handed over to the Japanese Imperial Navy, who in turn allowed the Minseibu, a civilian administration, to govern the day-to-day affairs of the island. The Minseibu, in contrast to the Japanese military, sought to create some stability on the island, as the Japanese intended to establish a long-term colonial presence.

Guam was renamed "Omiya Jima" or "Great Shrine Island" and all the villages were given new Japanese names as well. Teachers were brought in from elsewhere in Micronesia to open schools for the youth that focused heavily on teaching the Japanese language.

The Japanese proclaimed that Guam was part of a "Greater East-Asia Co-Prosperity Sphere," which would benefit the peoples of Asia and liberate them from the oppression of the West and the United States. Cultural exchange events were created to help familiarize Chamorros with Japanese traditions such as sumo wrestling matches and cherry blossom festivals.

The reality of the Japanese occupation was drastically different than the rhetoric. Private property rights were not respected and most Chamorro families lost their homes, and could also lose their food or cattle if a Japanese solider wanted it. Sexual assault by Japanese soldiers was something families constantly had to guard themselves against, with most hiding their young daughters away or disguising them as boys.

Work crews were created to farm for and feed the occupying Japanese.

Rations and wages were promised to support workers, but few wages and only the tiniest of rations were given. Furthermore, the Japanese sought to erase the American presence on the island by confiscating things written in English and also banning the use of the English language.

Although radios were confiscated, some Chamorros hid radio parts and would meet to assemble them. The Japanese provided propaganda on the war's progress, which Chamorros scarcely believed. These underground networks of radio listeners would gather to try to hear news from elsewhere in the world and would whisper word of America's forces moving back across the Pacific, ever closer to Guam.

January 1942 – March 1944 The island is placed under the control of the Japanese Imperial Navy. The Minseibu or civilian administration oversees the day-to-day affairs on the island.

January 1942 Guam is renamed "Omiya Jima" or "Great Shrine Island" and all the villages are also given Japanese names.

February 1942 Chamorros are first used for forced labor by the Japanese, most notably in agriculture to feed the occupying troops, but also in the construction of defense fortification. Rice farms are opened in Asai (Asan), Shoten (Piti), Suma (Sumay), Inada (Inarajan), Naka (Agat), Umata (Umatac) and Matsuyama (Malesso')

July 1942 Japanese teachers previously stationed in other islands in Micronesia are sent to Guam to fortify the island's school system. Instruction focuses primarily on learning the Japanese language, with daytime classes for youth and some night classes for adults.

December 10, 1942 The Japanese celebrate the one-year anniversary of taking Guam from the U.S. by holding a ceremony, which includes the dedication of a Shinto Shrine in Hagåtña and a parade.

October 1942 Six U.S. sailors flee into Guam's jungles rather than surrender to the Japanese. Three of them are found in September 1942 and two more are found in October 1942. They are all executed, leaving only one, George R. Tweed.

November 1942 Two Japanese Catholic priests are brought into the island to help smooth over relations between the Chamorro people and their new colonizers. Påle' Dueñas refers to them as "spies."

February 1943 Shoichi Yokoi, who would become famous for hiding in Guam's jungles for 27 years after the end of the war, is transferred to Guam.

August 27, 1943 The Japanese transport vessel *Tokai Maru* is sunk by the U.S. submarine *Snapper* in Apra Harbor.

October 1943 In preparation for a possible U.S. reinvasion, the Japanese begin to construct an airfield in Sumay. The residents had previously been expelled from the village by the Japanese. Sadly, even after the Americans return, they would still be prevented from going back.

June 15, 1944 the U.S. invasion of Saipan begins.

LABORING FROM DUSK TO DAWN

We worked in Malesso' for over a year when suddenly the authorities announced that males ages twelve to sixty-five were to be transported to Jalaguak, the present site of the Guam International Airport, to work in the construction of an airfield. So, one night, we were all loaded into a dump truck and travelled over two hours to reach Jalaguak.

Men from each of the villages were sent to work on the airstrip, with the Malesso' contingent assigned to the dusk-to-dawn shift. I remember there were but a few pieces of heavy equipment to spread the coral and compact the ground sturdy enough for the Japanese fighters and bombers to land on and take-off from.

During our off-duty hours, we were housed in a tent city about half a mile from the airfield. The labor conscripts came from different parts of the island and we shared our tents with people from all over. The insides of the huts were very hot and we had trouble sleeping despite long hours toiling in the airfield. To make matters worse, the latrines were nothing but trenches dug just outside the tents, which were open on all sides. The flies soon became a problem. After feeding on the waste matter in the trenches, they would come to roost on our faces, making sleep most difficult, if not impossible. I was with two of my uncles, Joaquin and Ignacio Manalisay Mata, and we got around the pest problem by having one of us shoo the flies off our faces while the other two tried to get some sleep.

We worked on the airfield, but on several occasions the Japanese would haul us by dump trucks to Piti to unload lighters. Japanese ships would be anchored at Apra Harbor and the Japanese would unload the cargo onto boats called lighters, small barges used to carry cargo from the ship directly to the beach because there were no piers built. Once on the beach, these lighters would be offloaded by stevedores.

I remember one particularly bad night for us. We had reached the Piti docks just after sunset and for a few hours there was a relative lull in activity. Around ten at night, lighters waiting to be offloaded had begun to line up and the Japanese again revealed their true colors. The Japanese apparently decided to off-load the lighters completely in several hours. With this in mind, three of them, whips in hand, took strategic places on the docks and would apply the whip on some of the stevedores they thought were not moving fast enough. I was young and fairly fit, so I had no trouble. But I saw a few of the elderly severely whipped because they did not or could not move fast enough.

We were returned to our oven-hut barracks, tired and hungry, around ten o'clock the next morning. I think they did this, not because we had worked long and hard, but because the ship was completely offloaded. We had only a few hours of sleep before we were again taken to the airfield to continue our work there.

I remember quite well the morning that the American carrier planes first strafed and bombed the airfield. It was around ten in the morning and I had just fallen asleep when Uncle Joaquin woke me. "Wake up, Boy, because there is something serious going on," he said. I sat up with a start and I looked west to the direction my uncle was pointing. The day was cloudy, but through breaks in the clouds I could see planes diving over what I thought to be Orote

Minseibu hospital staff and doctors with Chamorro nurses.

From the Collections of the Division of the Guam Museum, a division of the Department of Chamorro Affairs

Peninsula where the Japanese had completed an airfield. There were also numerous "puffs" of anti-aircraft shells fired by the Japanese. Almost immediately, everyone was awoken and became alert. We were all sure that the Americans were bombing and strafing the Orote airfield.

Suddenly and without warning, the roar of airplanes was above us. It was followed seconds later by the staccato of machine guns firing at us. At least that's what we thought. What was happening was that they were shooting at the airfield and discharging their guns above us. Other planes were bombing the airfield, located about a mile away, and we could see the bombs bursting all over the runway. The control tower was also hit and we could see a thick plume of smoke from the tower.

We did not stay around to see what was really going on. We knew the planes were American by the insignia on their wings and fuselages. Everyone in the barracks fled in every direction. Those of us from Malesso' took the road through Barrigåda and Mangilao, sleepy hamlets in those days, to the Chalan Påago crossroad and then turned south to Malesso'.

We were running uphill on the road leading to Yo'ña, about near where the new apartment buildings overlooking *Påago* Bay are now located. We didn't hear the plane coming at us, but suddenly we heard the "ra-ta-ta-ta-tat" of the machine guns. Bullets were flying all around us. Suddenly my Uncle Joaquin screamed, *"Ma danchi yu! Ma danchi yu!"*[6] He was lying on the ground writhing in pain, blood flowing down his neck from a bullet that grazed his skull. His right heel was shattered and he was bleeding profusely. But before we could attend to him, we heard the plane coming again and we all fled, half dragging my wounded uncle into an alcove that had

---

6 *Translation:* "I am hit! I am hit!"

been previously dug in the wall of the coral pit. The plane passed without shooting another round. The pilot must have thought that his human targets had all been killed.

One in our group took off his shirt and made a crude, tight tourniquet around my uncle's ankle and after a few minutes, the bleeding stopped. Since he was in no condition to continue his walk, my other uncle and I took turns carrying him, piggy-back, until we reached Malo'lo' where Uncle Joaquin's godmother, *Tan Chong "Daña"* Meno lived. By the time we reached his godmother's place, my wounded uncle was feverish and was talking incoherently. One look at him and *Tan Chong* pronounced that Uncle Joaquin was in no condition to travel any further. "You go on to Malesso'," she said, "and tell my *kumaire* that I'll take care of my godson and I will allow him to continue to Malesso' only after he has recovered completely." After about a month, Uncle Joaquin was nursed back to health and we took a *karetan guaka* to fetch him back to Malesso'.

Our relative freedom after fleeing Jalaguak was short-lived. Less than a week after we had come home, notice was given that all males over the age of eleven must assemble at the Japanese headquarters in Malesso'. The Japanese revived the labor battalions that had been dissolved and all able-bodied men and boys were quickly transported to work at the Jalaguak airfield. Labor Battalion Six worked closest to the beach (in *Sumai Malesso'*) and from sun-up to sun-down, we felled coconut trees in order to build obstacles to tanks and amphibious vehicles that may be used in an American invasion.

Our labor battalion was headed by an Army lieutenant, "Lieutenant Sato" (his pseudonym since I forgot what his real name was). He was young, in his late twenties or early thirties. He and the other ten soldiers in his group all lived in a substantial *låncho* (ranch house) that was expropriated from its owner, *Tun* Juan Trinidad Duenas Torres, my grandmother's brother.

This lieutenant was the first Japanese to show kindness and consideration to us. He did hit me sharply on the head with his fist when at one time I was slow to take cover at the approach of an American plane; at that time the Americans were shooting everything that moved, humans and animals. "*Baga mono*, you fool," he practically screamed at me. "By not taking cover immediately, you are endangering not only your life but the lives of those around you. Just make sure that you don't do that again or your punishment will be more severe." For hitting me, he later apologized, an action that was so alien to the Japanese occupiers.

"Lt. Sato" knew some English, which he used to convey his work orders to us. One day he made a strange and interesting proposition to me, "You teach me English and I'll teach you Japanese." I didn't ask him why he wanted to learn since I was afraid there might be a misunderstanding between the two of us and I never did learn why. In any event, every night after supper and after the Japanese had taken their communal bath in preheated water in a fifty-gallon drum, I would come to Sato's barracks for the English-Japanese instruction period.

One evening after our labor battalion had been building fortifications for about a month, we were visited at our *låncho* by a messenger from the Japanese headquarters in Malesso' to tell us that all males between the ages of fifteen and sixty-five were to report to the Japanese headquarters the following evening at eight. We were being transported back to Jalaguak to resume work on the airfield. I remember there was a lull in the American air bombardments and apparently the Japanese had decided to resume work on the airfield. Lt. Sato listened intently when I told him what the new orders were for us. He then said for me to report to him as usual the next morning.

When I arrived at headquarters the next morning, Sato was waiting for me. He was wearing a clean uniform, beribboned, with a saber in a scabbard hanging by his side. He was also wearing clean white gloves and his boots had been shined. The lieutenant looked serious and glum. "Come with me," he said.

We hiked the two miles to the Malesso' headquarters of the Japanese. The five-or-six-soldier contingent at the headquarters apparently saw the lieutenant coming. Realizing that the oncoming officer out-ranked them all, there was a wild scramble to form a line, with one or two trying to tuck in their shirttails before the lieutenant reached them.

Before even reaching the line of Japanese soldiers, who were now so intensely listening to the Sato's words and nodding their heads and exclaiming "*Hai, hai.*" Sato was addressing them in a guttural voice the gist of which I understood a little. They were being told that I was not to go the next evening with the contingent of Chamorros to the Jalaguak airfield. After delivering his edict, he turned around and we started our trek back to *Sumai Malesso'*.

We continued work under Sato for a number of days when the lieutenant and his group suddenly disappeared. They were apparently ordered to move and we were not told of the new development. Our labor contingent continued to build beach fortifications under a new group of Japanese.

Two incidents under these new Japanese stood out in my mind and in the minds of my other Chamorro compatriots. First, one afternoon a squad of Japanese soldiers, without warning, set up what we learned was a mortar apparatus and started to fire rounds of the ammunition towards the surrounding hill. They fired without even trying to determine whether people were living beyond those hills. But most of the projectiles were duds and after the failed firings, one of the Chamorro boys (a smart aleck I'd say) muttered under his breath: "And they expect to win the war with this?"

Second, while we were working on the beach erecting barriers of

The *kampanåyon*, built in 1910, remains standing in the village of Malesso' up until today.

From the Collections of the Division of the Guam Museum, a division of the Department of Chamorro Affairs

Galaide' such as these were used often in the village of Malesso' in order to fish in the lagoon and travel to nearby *Dåno'*.

From the Collections of the Division of the Guam Museum,
a division of the Department of Chamorro Affairs

coconut-tree logs one afternoon, we saw from the distance a swarm of planes above *Dåno'*. The planes were weaving, with some of them climbing, others diving in what was evidently a dog-fight between a dozen warplanes. The action was too far away for us to identify the combatants but we figured that surely the fight was between American and Japanese warplanes. The fight continued on for several minutes or so when suddenly we saw a plane climb straight up, pause momentarily and then plunge, tail first, in slow-motion, into the waters below. The action was too far away from us to see the splash as the craft hit the water. Suddenly, the Japanese with us erupted in applause. And just as suddenly a wag among us muttered under his breath: "How do these devils know that it was not a Japanese plane that fell?" We had to suppress a chuckle for fear of being beaten for ever thinking that an Imperial warplane had been destroyed by the Americans.

One day before quitting time, we were told that we were to carry ammunition from a depot in *As Liyo* (a locale outside Malesso') to Otdot. There were about fifteen of us and we started the ammunition-carrying trek that same night. Perhaps because I knew a little more Japanese than the rest of the other men and could act as interpreter, the Japanese *taicho* chose me as his valet and all I did was carry his briefcase and some personal belongings.

We had just started to climb the winding hills just northeast of Inalåhan when one of the men fell to the ground clutching his belly, screaming and calling out to his mother in pain: *"Ai Nåna, ai Nåna."*

The *taicho* looked at the man and then looked at me. "What's the matter with him?" he asked. I shrugged my shoulder and said, "I don't know, *wakara nai*."

A few moments later when the Japanese was convinced that the man was indeed in pain and could no longer continue the trek, he said to the man, "Go home, go."

In a flash, the man was up and running. At that, the rest of the men could not resist chuckling for they were convinced his act was all part of a ruse. "He got away so fast that we couldn't even see the whites of his feet," one said. This was the man who had earlier claimed that he was hit on the neck with a machete by one with whom he was arguing. We shall meet this same man for a third and last time later on in our story.

When we reached Otdot the following day, the group was allowed to return home except that the *taicho*, who had supervised our trek the night before, had chosen me for his valet and ordered me to stay.

The Japanese had transformed Otdot into an ammunition depot. Munitions were housed in bunkers all around the depot (some were piled haphazardly on the ground) and the soldiers stationed there were tasked with guarding the depot.

The Japanese did not engage in daytime activities, cooking most especially, for fear that the smoke would be quickly spotted from the air by the American warplanes, which now had complete control of the skies. It was a nerve-wracking existence for me (and for the Japanese, I suppose). The American planes would start their daily attacks on the airfield and in the process making it seem that they were attacking us.

"I need to get out of this place before the Americans bomb it and we all get killed," I told myself. I told the *taicho* that when I left my mother four days ago, she was ill and asked if he would let me go find out how she was. Surprisingly, he readily agreed. He ordered one of his aides to bring him a piece of cloth on which he wrote, in *kanji*, a pass which he cautioned me to pin on my clothes at all times. I then made a wild dash to the highway that would take me south to my home and family. I had gone but a few yards when he called me back. "What now?!" I thought. "Did he change his mind and now wants me to continue living with them in this dangerous place?" But he ordered the aide to fill my knapsack with uncooked rice. "Take this for your sick mother and maybe she will get well after eating it," he said.

I then made a dash to the highway and started running south toward Yo'ña, Inalåhan, and eventually, Malesso'. But I wasn't running on the highway but on the roadside, which was pretty well covered by tall vegetation and I was hidden from the trigger-happy American fliers.

When I came to Yo'ña, at the place where the Catholic Church is now, I was accosted by three armed Japanese who wanted to know what I was doing on the road at that time of the day. As I started to explain, they espied the *kanji* pass pinned to my shirt and they seemed to calm down after they read it. They then allowed me to continue but warned that I needed to be careful for "the American devils will shoot from the air at anything that moved."

All the time I was in Otdot, I kept worrying that my family (and everyone in the village) had been herded by the Japanese to God knows where. A few days before our munitions-carrying trek, the Japanese had dismissed us from work well after dark. On our way home to our respective *lånchos*, we met what seemed to be the entire population of the village. When my mother spotted me, she started to hug me, crying that they didn't know where they were being taken. She said that they had been preparing to go to bed when they received an order for everyone to assemble at the Japanese headquarters in Malesso'. Once there, the villagers were then ordered to start their trek eastward toward Inalåhan. When we met them, they were being herded by armed, growling Japanese guards. One of them prodded my mother to keep moving when he saw us talking.

When I reached home, I found that the sleeping mats, pillows and sheets were on the floor, all indicating that my family members were indeed in bed, or were in the process of going to sleep, when they received orders by the Japanese compelling them to go to their headquarters in Malesso'. In the kitchen, I found some cooked bananas and breadfruit, but I had lost my appetite and started to weep bitterly upon thinking how the Japanese were cruelly treating us—my family and my aged grandmother most especially. This renewed and intensified hatred and contempt for the Japanese was to serve my psyche well during the violent incident that I participated in the day after I had reached the Atåte camp from the forced march to Otdot, and the fear and anxiety that had gripped me throughout my forced four-day stay there.

The forced trek to Inalåhan that night was aborted by the Japanese as the group neared Inalåhan. They were suddenly ordered to turn around and go home and to be ready to follow the next Japanese orders to go someplace of the enemy's choosing. It was near dawn when I was awakened by my family returning from that God-awful, senseless and dehumanizing trek imposed on my helpless people by a sadistic enemy.

With these thoughts in my mind, my plan after leaving Otdot was to reach Malesso'. If I did not find my family there, I was certain to find someone who could tell me where our people were.

MY SEARCH FOR ATÅTE

I met the first Chamorros on the road when I reached Tinaga just before Inalåhan. There were three of them and they all appeared startled to see a bare-footed and ill-clad Chamorro running toward them. Even before they asked, I began telling them who I was, how the Japanese, five days prior, forced about thirty of us from Malesso' to carry munitions to Otdot. The others were then dismissed to go home, but I was forced to stay with the Japanese as a valet to the ranking officer of the contingent guarding the munitions at Otdot. I explained I was released just that morning and I was now on my way to my village, although I strongly suspected that the Malesso' people were not in their respective homes, but rather they were herded some place.

After telling them my story, I asked if they knew where the Malesso' people were. "In Atåte," they responded almost in unison. Although I didn't know where the place Atåte was exactly, the name didn't ring unfamiliar. My late father was an avid wild game hunter and I heard how he and his hunting partner, Antonio Leon Guerrero Cruz, would go to the place called Atåte where wild game (deer, wild pigs, fowl) were plentiful and where they would place *nåsan uhang* and *nåsan asuli*[7] in the river that flows through the place.

---

7   Traps of woven bamboo strips designed to catch shrimp and eels

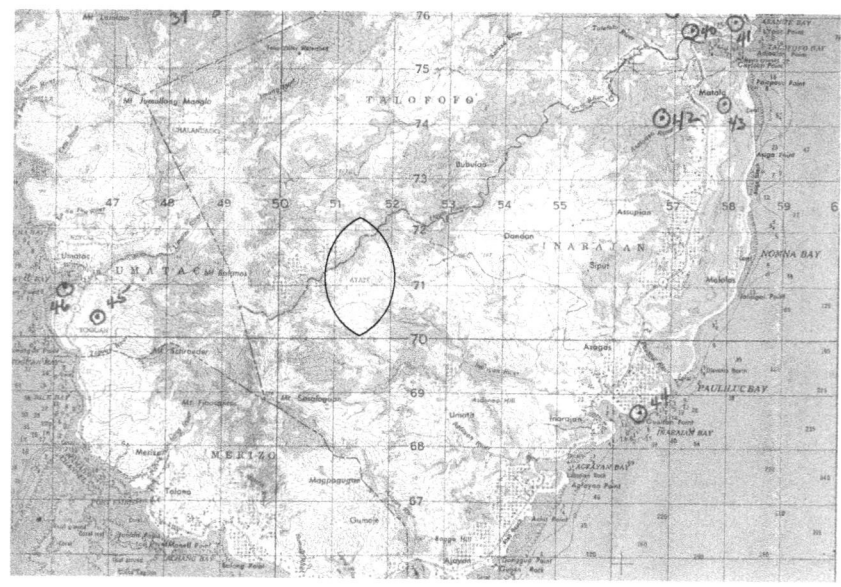

Atåte can be found on the edge of Malesso' and Inalåhan.

From the Collections of the Micronesian Area Research Center

On learning that my people were in that place, I changed my original plan about going all the way to Malesso' and instead focused on going to Atåte. It was a few hours before dark. When my Inalåhan friends realized I was planning to enter the jungle and continue the search for my people, they suggested that I spend the night in their camp and in the morning accompany the group that was to leave camp to search for food in the jungle. They would then point out more precisely where Atåte was.

The sun was already up the following morning when the group of two *karabao*, three men and I started out. After plodding for about an hour (at an exasperatingly slow speed for me) we reached a precipice from where we could see the lush, green valley below. The caravan stopped.

"There is Atåte," said one of the men, pointing to no one place in particular in the valley below. Their ambiguity did not particularly faze me, for during the previous night, I was imbued with one idea: find the river that flows through the valley, follow it, upstream most likely, and find your people. I knew that to find the river, which flows north to south, one must travel in a westerly direction perpendicular to the river's flow and that the sun's movement from east to west would be my guide. But I also had to remember that at this time of the year (it was during the rainy season), when there is an over-cast throughout the day and the sun is blotted out, one must depend on one's instincts for direction.

I thanked the men and had just started my dash to enter the jungle when one of them called me using the affectionate name for Jose in Chamorro: "*Peling*, take this. You'll need it." He was holding a machete.

Especially in the south of the island, Guam's jungles—"boonies" to some are nearly impenetrable, largely because of the dense and ubiquitous undergrowth, mostly of the wild *lemon de china*, a squat plant with deep green leaves and sharp thorns. It produces perennial berries, acidly sweet in taste and bright red in color when ripened.

I had my first sustenance in many a day soon after I had entered the boonies: the *lemon de china* berries and ripe, wild papayas. Afterwards, I continued my trek, sometimes in a plodding fashion, sometimes at a quicker pace when the thick undergrowth, (or its lack thereof) allowed me. And all the time I was striving to move in a due westwardly direction assisted by the movements of the sun.

I FOUND MY PEOPLE

I, of course, didn't have a timepiece to allow me to determine how long I had been in the jungle in search of my people. But suddenly, there it was, right in front of me. I found a wide swath. I estimated that it was about some forty-feet wide, of trodden undergrowth trampled no doubt by countless, tired feet of frightened people herded by the diabolical Japanese to the camp that couldn't be far away. I shouted for joy and began running, knowing that in a few moments I would find my people.

Soon, I began to hear voices and suddenly the camp appeared before me. Situated on a rise on the riverbank, the camp was dotted, haphazardly as it were, by bamboo and coconut leaf huts that were hastily erected to keep out the rains. In the middle of the camp were two large tarpaulin tents, one for sleeping quarters for the enemy; the other, a storage tent for their ill-gotten gains.

Mere minutes after I had reached the camp, I was besieged by young women who anxiously asked where I was coming from and whether I had met their Vicente, or their Juan, or their Francisco, or their Jose. It appeared that six days prior, the Japanese had rounded up the youngest, biggest, healthiest and strongest of the village's men and marched them away under heavily armed guard. None of them had been seen ever since.

I told the women that I was coming from Otdot and Inalåhan, and that no, I had not met any of their husbands. It appeared that most everyone in the camp had heard about a massacre that occurred at Tinta, and the women had begun to suspect that something similarly dreadful had happened to their husbands. After learning that I had not seen or met their husbands, they did not wail nor moan, but rather they wept and sobbed silently. "Such brave women," I thought.

THE TINTA MASSACRE

The Japanese had constructed a list—a blacklist, if you will—of people they thought were subversives. This list was made of fathers or male siblings of villagers who had joined the U.S. Navy, people they thought had no proper respect for the Japanese and others who were placed on the list for various reasons. During the second night of the people's forced march to Atåte, those on the blacklist were separated from the group and forced into a bunker in Tinta, on the eastern side of *Geus* Valley. The Japanese then started to lob hand grenades into the huddled, frightened mass. Afterwards, the Japanese, led by a man named Ohashi, went around administering the *coup de grâce*[8] on those who showed signs of still being alive.

One of the victims who survived the initial blasts was Maria Lukban Mesa. Maria, a Filipina, was married to a Chamorro, Tomas Mesa. After moving to Guam in 1928, Maria had eight children with Tomas. Maria was a university graduate and was proficient in English, the language of instruction in Guam's schools. She later became principal of the Dedidu school. Two years before the war, she was appointed principal of the Malesso' school. In the meanwhile, her husband had moved to Manila to attend dental school, and so he wasn't on island when the Japanese invaded Guam.

---

8   A final blow or shot given to kill a wounded person.

Chamorro elders strolling along the main street of prewar Malesso'.

From the Collections of the Division of the Guam Museum, a division of the Department of Chamorro Affairs

From the beginning, Mrs. Mesa, in despair at the Japanese takeover of the island, rebelled against the invaders and was beaten a number of times. Because of her rebellious nature, she was probably at the top of the enemy's black list. And so she was with the group of people who were herded into the Tinta bunk.

The rest of the people of Malesso' were trying to find adequate shelter on the western side of *Geus* Valley when they heard explosions coming from the eastern side. The explosions they heard were grenades thrown by the Japanese in their effort to kill the blacklisted Chamorros.

Mrs. Mesa, although wounded by the grenades, was still alive when the Japanese, led by Ohashi, entered the bunker. Ohashi's aim was to leave no survivors. According to others who survived the attack, some people who weren't wounded or were only slightly wounded, pretended to play dead or pulled the dead over them so that the Japanese could not see them. They heard Mrs. Mesa pleading for her life. Instead Ohashi plunged his sword into her chest.

Thinking that everyone had been killed, the Japanese left the bunker and later took shelter in a nearby grass hut during a heavy and prolonged downpour. It was during this unguarded moment when the victims, who were unhurt, only slightly wounded or more severely wounded but could still move, crept out of the bunker and fled to the safety of the nearby jungle. One unwounded survivor was Tomas Espinosa Cruz, *Tun Tomas Domma*, whose flat-bed truck hauled fruits and vegetables to the Hagåtña farmers' market before the war. He was also the father of a U.S. Navy sailor. *Tun Tomas* had managed to reach Atåte a few days after escaping Tinta and pulled his family out of the camp.

HISTORICAL NOTES

FINAL TRAGEDIES AND TRAUMA

For most of the 32-month occupation by the Japanese, Chamorros did their best to avoid their new occupier. They stayed away from villages and worked their ranches, minimizing contact with the Japanese as much as possible. Despite this distance, every Chamorro felt the hardship in different ways. Many did not get enough to eat and were worked to exhaustion by the occupiers. There were constant threats of violence. Even if a family was fortunate enough not to suffer violence directly, they lived in constant fear of it.

Things worsened as the U.S. moved closer to the Mariana Islands and began to attack Saipan and Tinian to the north. As U.S. ships blockaded Guam and American bombs began to fall on the island, the most traumatic and terrifying chapter of the occupation began. Hundreds of Chamorros during this period were massacred and thousands were forced to march to a concentration camp in the island's center at Manenggon.

Some of these massacres were carried out to prevent Chamorros from being able to assist the U.S. military with their knowledge of Japanese defenses and fortifications. Others were done out of cruel spite, simply to hurt the Chamorro people and vent Japanese frustration over lost imperial ambitions and a war against the United States that they certainly were not going to win.

February 1944 The first American planes in over two years are sighted dogfighting with Japanese planes over Orote Peninsula.

March – July 1944 The Japanese Imperial Army returns to Guam and assumes control, leading to the most violent and traumatic period for the Chamorro people as the Japanese prepare for the impending U.S. attack.

July 8, 1944 American warships commence a 13-day bombardment of the island prior to invasion.

July 9, 1944 After 24 days of fighting, American troops declare Saipan officially taken from the Japanese.

July 10, 1944 The only remaining American holdout George Tweed is picked up by the U.S. Navy Destroyer the U.S.S. *McCall*, after being hidden by Chamorro families for more than two-and-a-half years.

July 11, 1944 Orders are given to round up all Chamorros and force them to march to a concentration camp in Manenggon. Some are taken to other concentration camps around the island.

July 12, 1944 Påle' Jesus Baza Dueñas, the leader of Guam's Catholic Church during the war, is executed along with his nephew and two others in Ta'i, Mangilao.

July 15 – 16 In the village of Malesso', two groups of thirty each are taken to Japanese bomb shelters or bokkongo at Tinta and Fåha. After being told they were chosen for special work details, the Japanese instead attempt to massacre them. Fourteen of the 30 brought to Tinta survive the massacre. None of the 30 taken to Fåha survive.

July 20, 1944 The Japanese round up a group of more than a dozen men and women in Hagåtña and execute them. Miraculously two survive, Beatrice Flores and Juan Cabrera, both of whom bore deep scars on their necks and backs from Japanese swords and bayonets.

THE MASSACRE OF THE JAPANESE AT ATÅTE

At the Atåte camp, I found a shack that had been built by my uncle, Vicente Manalisay Mata. *Tatan Ben*, as we called him, was one of the men who disappeared at the hands of the Japanese. It was late in the afternoon when my mother and my two older sisters returned from a food-gathering foray in the jungle. Their find included pitifully few breadfruit and wild taro, *piga*, and food that would last us for a day or two. But they were overjoyed when they saw me, because they all thought that somehow the worst had happened to me since my other companions had all returned from Otdot without me.

Shortly after my return, the Japanese gave an order: first thing the next morning, all men and boys were to go to the rice depot about a mile away and haul the grains to Atåte. Additionally, teen-aged boys were to go to Malesso' to fetch live chickens.

After a breakfast of boiled breadfruit and wild taro from the night before, I started my trek to *Tingting Hånom*. The depot was on an embankment overlooking the river, which at this point became a small waterfall. The water produced a tinkling sound that bespoke its name *Tingting Hånom*, "tinkling waters." There were about fifty or more sacks of rice stacked in the tent, and each sack I estimated to weigh fifty pounds or more. There were three armed soldiers guarding the supply and they allowed two carriers for each bag. Jose Acfalle Baza, "*Hosen Toro*" was my partner and we wasted no time leaving with our haul.

After about twenty minutes on the trail, we decided to stop for a rest and discuss. a plan that we both had almost simultaneously conceived. We decided not to deliver our load to Atåte until just before dark so that we wouldn't have to go back to *Tingting Hånom* for a second load. We would then be very tired and hungry since we did not expect to eat anything that day. So we veered off the trail and started to search for a dry spot, which would provide adequate shelter from the near-incessant rain. We found a clump of sword grass whose leaves formed a canopy under which the ground was dry. We then gathered dry leaves for bedding and soon we were sleeping as comfortably as the circumstance allowed.

We were awakened a short time later by voices coming from the trail a short distance away. Getting up to investigate, we saw a strange and alarming sight: a group of men and boys, some of whom were carrying rifles and swords. Chamorros just didn't go around carrying arms like what we were seeing. We asked one of the men in the group, Ramon Baza Acfalle—*Ramon Pagalai*—what was going on.

"The Americans have landed at Cocos Island. We're now going on to kill the Japanese at Atåte," he told us. He also told us that the three Japanese guarding the rice depot as well as the one who had earlier gone to Malesso' had all been killed and added, "We are now going to kill the Japanese at Atåte."

Earlier, Jose Soriano Reyes, "*Tonko*" led Patricio Taijeron and the Nangauta brothers, Jose and Mariano, in the attack on the three Japanese guarding the rice depot. On entering the rice depot, *Tonko* immediately hit the Japanese sitting atop a pile of rice sacks with his fist, knocking him unconscious. This was the signal for his three accomplices, the Nangauta brothers and Taijeron, to attack and subdue the other two Japanese. All three Japanese were then dragged to the river below where they were stoned to death. Taking the rifle of one of the dead Japanese, *Tonko* then ambushed and shot to death the Japanese who was returning from Malesso' with the young boys. Sadly, the shot also hit two boys following behind the Japanese, Gregorio Chargualaf Santiago and Jose Taijeron Garrido. Santiago was hit in the stomach and died later that day, but Garrido survived with a hand wound.

Tonko did recruit others, such as Vicente Meno Meno, Nicolas Ada Chargualaf and Juan Naputi for that assault, but later changed his mind, because he felt that it was too risky to storm the heavily armed enemy.

There were about twenty men and boys on the trail to Atåte when *Pop Tonko* outlined his plan. Two volunteers, Juan Cruz Borja or *Tun Juan Pelu* and Juan Meno Garrido or *Juan Bulu* were to take the bag of rice to the tent's door. *Bulu* would then call out the Japanese, and when one came out, Garrido was to hit him with his fist. Meanwhile, all who were taking part in the assault were to stay out of sight and rush the tent only after Garrido had hit the Japanese. And soon after the fight started, the teen-aged boys, who had earlier accompanied the Japanese to Malesso', were to seize the rifles that were neatly stacked by the tent's wall.

When Garrido and Borja reached the entrance, they let down their cargo and called the Japanese. One of them soon emerged. But Garrido hesitated. The Japanese then looked out and apparently saw us, now standing in the open, not carrying rice bags and apparently with fear ridden faces. Now thoroughly alarmed, he started yelling, "You, and you, and you, where are your rice bags? *Kioski!!!*"

It was then that *Tonko*, standing behind a fern tree, yelled, "*Bulu, hafa depotsi para un cho'gue? Pañiti enao osino Hågu bai hu paki!*"[9] It all happened in mere seconds and then *Bulu* reared and let go a haymaker. The Japanese soldier crumbled.

---

9   *Translation:* "Bulu, what are you supposed to do? Hit him or I'll shoot you instead."

That was the sign we were waiting for. But before we reached the tent door, which was only wide enough to admit but a few people at a time, a woman behind us, now immediately aware of what was happening, yelled, "*Ayugue unu kumekefalågu. Dulalak ya en pino', et Diablo.*"[10] There was also this other woman who quickly understood what was happening and started to wail: "*Ai, hafa na en che'che'gue enao? Siempre manmapuno' hit på'go todudus.*"[11]

The Japanese was crawling sideways—like a crab. He was naked except for a bright red loincloth. Following the first hits on the Japanese (most of them wielded by my friend, *Jose Toro*) the Japanese assumed a fetal position, lying on his side, his legs flexed to his abdomen, his arms drawn over his ears to protect his head. He then started to whimper, "*Hafa taotao cho'gue este?*"[12] Incredibly, he was speaking not only in Chamorro but he appeared to be absolving himself of the deadly acts at Tinta and Fåha—as if he were simply following orders and should not be held accountable for his actions.

A few more hits and he went limp at which time the woman behind us yelled, "*I damot-ña, galuti i damot-ña.*"[13] That was unnecessary for the man was already dead, terribly and finally dead, with parts of his brain splattered all over the surrounding vegetation.

Years later at a party, *Toro* and I were talking about that particular part of our assault on the Japanese at Atåte. I said that he probably wielded the most number of lethal blows on that particular Japanese. *Toro* took a deep drag on his cigarette, gulped a mouthful of beer and said: "He deserved to die. He was one of those who killed my uncle and his son, my cousin, who had joined the U.S. Navy just before the start of the war."

---

10 *Translation:* "There is one trying to get away. Go after him and kill him, the devil."
11 *Translation:* "Ai, why are you doing this? Now they are going to kill us all."
12 *Translation:* "Why are you people doing this?)"
13 *Translation:* "His balls, hit his balls."

THE JAPANESE ARE CHOKED TO DEATH

When we were finished with that Japanese man, we then turned our attention to the activity inside the tent. But before we could rush in, the structure collapsed from the sheer activity inside it. Even after the collapse, we could detect continuous activity. Suddenly it stopped. A short time later, the Chamorro warriors began to emerge one by one. After they had all gotten out and were accounted for, *Pop Tonko* ordered that the dead Japanese men be dragged out and lined up in front of the tent. No weapons were noted to have been used. Each and every Japanese had apparently been strangled to death. Six dead Japanese were counted, but *Tonko* was alarmed that the diabolical Ohashi wasn't one of them.

"Where is Ohashi?" he asked, almost shouting. No one seemed to know. Ramona Cruz San Nicolas later described the scene of his escape. She said that she was in the river washing clothes when suddenly she saw Ohashi, ashen faced and holding a bare sword, leaping across the river. He later confronted two elderly sisters, Petronila and Andrea Acfalle, who were living in a make-shift hut by the trail. Petronila's hand was almost severed when she tried to deflect the sword blow by Ohashi. She survived but Andrea later died of a severe wound to her neck inflicted by the desperately fleeing Japanese man. Ohashi later reached the Inalåhan camp, where he warned the Chamorros not to go to the Malesso' Atåte camp, because the people there were murderous.

The Chamorros suffered only one casualty. Juan Cruz Borja (the co-conspirator of *Juan Bulu*, remember?) sustained a cut to his right forearm, a wound inflicted by Ohashi after the Japanese had managed to get a hold of his saber. But Ohashi realized that he and his saber were no match for the enraged and emboldened Chamorros now attacking the Japanese and so he fled.

Borja's anger had not subsided when he viewed the dead Japanese now lying in a neat row in front of the collapsed tent. He then grabbed a knife and started stabbing the corpses, crying with rage as he did so. And Vicente Nangauta (*Bisentin Chedi*), not known for his mental prowess, was hacking the corpses one by one with a mattock, muttering, "*Hu puno' hao, hu puno' hao,*"[14] as he struck the blows.

One would expect that the mood of the people, after their deadly captors had all been killed, would have been celebratory with dancing, singing, back-slapping and joyously embracing each other. But the crowd was quiet, somber, reflective and frightened, perhaps. I attribute this to at least two factors: our religious upbringing ("Thou shalt not kill") and the possibility of a quick and violent retaliation by the enemy, especially since Ohashi, the architect of the Tinta and Fåha massacres, had escaped.

---

14   Translation: *"I kill you, I kill you."*

SIX VOLUNTEERS TO CONTACT THE AMERICANS STEPPED UP

Some of our people were not carrying rice supplies from *Tingting Hånom* that day but instead were foraging for food. The foraging party included my mother and two of my older sisters. Another was Jesus Barcinas, a prewar school teacher who was married to my father's sister. He returned to camp at the time we were all milling around the dead Japanese.

Barcinas was alarmed that we had killed the enemy and was afraid (like many of us) of retaliation from the Japanese. He surveyed the dead Japanese on the ground and blurted out *"Håyi chumo'gue este?"*[15] to no one in particular. He received no answer. He then recovered his composure and said: "We need to contact the Americans to protect us from the Japanese. I need volunteers".

Five of us stepped forward: Antonio Leon Guerrero Cruz, Joaquin Chargualaf Manalisay, Juan Meno Garrido, Juan Atoigue Cruz, and me. With Barcinas as our leader, we prepared to move out immediately. The people also had decided to abandon the Atåte camp with some moving to *Finile*, some to *As Båyu*, and the rest to *Halaohan*.

---

15   *Translation:* "Who did this?"

AN ADDITIONAL DEAD JAPANESE

Early in the morning on the day of the attack, Ohashi wanted to send a message to a Japanese official in the Hågat area. He chose one of his men, who in turn chose two Chamorros to accompany him: Jesus Reyes Quinene and Vicente Garrido Cruz. After hiking for about two hours, they reached a Hågat overlook from where they saw an incredible sight: hundreds of ships, the American invasion fleet, no doubt. The Japanese turned ashen-faced while the two Chamorros tried to conceal their joy at this sudden turn of events. The trio then turned around and started their trek back to Atåte.

At Atåte, they found the dead Japanese and the camp deserted. The Japanese had thought that the Americans had reached the camp and they themselves had killed the Japanese. A Japanese man then looked for and found a shovel. He asked Quinene and Cruz to help him dig a hole. After the hole was sufficiently deep, the Japanese told the two men to stay as far away for he would then climb into the hole and blow himself up. He asked the two men to cover up the hole with dirt. Quinene and Cruz retreated to some distance from the hole and soon they heard a click followed by an explosion. They returned to the hole to find the man mangled and thoroughly dead. "One of our better jobs that day was sealing the tomb of the Japanese," Quinene later told me.

IN SEARCH OF HELP FROM THE AMERICANS

Because Antonio Cruz was thoroughly familiar with the topography of the *Finile* area, he unerringly led us to the hut where Charfauros was. There was a nauseating stench of decaying flesh that assaulted our sense of smell as we approached the hut.

"Manuel, Manuel," Cruz called out, not too kindly, I might say. "This is Antonio Cruz, *Antonion Ana*. We have killed all the Japanese at Atåte and are now on our way to find the Americans for help."

"*Na'gimen yu', na'gimen yu'*."[16] Charfauros weakly replied.

At that, Garrido quickly climbed a coconut tree and cut down a bunch of *månha*[17] and deftly fashioned a few of them for drinking.

"Our people are now moving out of Atåte to other places where the Japanese won't find them," Cruz further told Charfauros. "They know you're here and your family will find you."

Charfauros survived his wound and for many years he was principal of the post-war Malesso' elementary school. Upon his retirement, he moved to California where he died in 1987 at the age of ninety.

Before the volunteer group left Atåte to try to contact the Americans for help, it was decided that the quickest way to contact the Americans, whose warships were then plying the Guam waters

---

16   *Translation:* "Give me drink, give me drink."
17   Young coconuts

Malesso' fishermen preparing to enter the Dåno' lagoon and cast their nets.

*From the Collections of the Division of the Guam Museum,
a division of the Department of Chamorro Affairs*

with impunity, was to find a craft to get us to Dåno' that night and in the morning row out to the high seas where the group hoped to be picked up by one of the American warships. But to do all this, we needed to find a craft large enough to carry the six of us.

Vicente Acfalle Champaco, *Tun Bisenten Karabao*, had built himself a large out-rigger canoe—an ocean-going canoe, as a matter of fact—and one of the things we had to do that night was to find *Tun Bisente's* canoe. Unfortunately for *Tun Bisente*, a member of the Guam Insular Guard, a quasi-military force, he was one of those who was blacklisted and did not survive the Tinta massacre.

After a short search on the beach, we found the craft high and dry and apparently in ship-shape condition to carry us to Dåno' that night. Finding the craft structurally sound with the outrigger still firmly tied to its body, we launched the canoe. After fashioning a couple paddles from stems of coconut leaves (only two wooden paddles were found in the craft) we were well on our way to Dåno'.

It was a clear, moonless night and the stars appeared brighter and even lower. It was all too surreal. We were in the midst of apparent calm, peace and serenity whereas only a few hours earlier human beings were being killed by the oppressed rising up in a bid for freedom from their sadistic and murderous oppressors.

After reaching Dåno', we hauled the canoe ashore and posited it under a canopy of overhanging trees. We re-inspected the craft for its seaworthiness before loading it with ripe, wild papayas and *månha*. We then tried to catch some sleep, but I don't think any of us slept amid a nervous anticipation of an uncertain morning that would soon be upon us.

HISTORICAL NOTES

GUAM'S LIBERATION BEGINS IN ATÅTE

While Americans were circling the island, bombarding and flattening it in preparation for their reinvasion, the group of Malesso' men led by Jose "Tonko" Reyes attacked their Japanese captors, killing 10 of them and liberating those kept in the concentration camp at Atåte.

The next day, on July 21, 1944, the U.S. reinvasion began with Marines hitting the beaches at Asan and Hågat. The fighting was fierce, but the Japanese knew their defense was hopeless. On the night of July 25, 1944, Japanese forces, hoping to break the U.S. beachhead at Asan, sent thousands of men into the frontlines in a series of seven banzai or suicidal charges. They were unsuccessful.

With each passing day of fighting, the U.S. pushed the Japanese further north, and by the end of July, succeeded in securing Orote Peninsula and Hagåtña. The last command post for the Japanese was set up in Yigo, in the Mataguac area. When U.S. forces entered the area prior to the Japanese surrender, they found dozens of bodies of beheaded Chamorros.

On August 10, 1944, the U.S. announced that combat on Guam had ended and the island was theirs once again. Japanese stragglers, refusing to surrender, would remain in hiding for decades. In the late 1940s, a group of Chamorro hunters and soldiers called the Guam Combat Patrol was formed to catch and kill hundreds of stragglers. The last holdout, Shoichi Yokoi, was found by two Chamorro hunters in January 1972.

As the fighting subsided, Chamorros rejoiced at the return of the

United States, although life would never return to its prewar normal. Hagåtña had been almost completely destroyed in the fighting, and while most Chamorros had lived there prior to the war, nearly all would be displaced into other villages. Thousands of Chamorro families would be unable to return to their homes or farms in the postwar years, as the U.S. military seized them in order to create larger, more modern bases on the island. The entire village of Sumay was lost, first taken by the Japanese and then again by the U.S. following the war.

On July 21, 1945, the Chamorro people held their first annual commemoration of Liberation Day. This first commemoration featured a mass and a lukao (procession), honoring and remembering those who died in the Japanese occupation of Guam. For the second commemoration in 1946, Liberation Day would take on a more militaristic and patriotic tone, featuring more American flags and a parade of U.S. military forces.

July 20, 1944 After learning about the massacres of their families and friends, a group of men led by Jose "Tonko" Reyes attack their Japanese captors at Atåte, killing 10 of them and liberating themselves prior to the American reinvasion.

July 21, 1944 The U.S. reinvasion of the island begins, with Marines attacking at beaches in Asan and Hågat.

July 23, 1944 Close-to-100 young Chamorros are taken by the Japanese into caves at Fena prior to the American re-invasion. As the Japanese defense of Guam beings to fail, the troops massacre more than 30 with bayonets and grenades. Many of the young women are raped prior to being killed.

July 24, 1944 U.S. forces invade Tinian and secure the island within 8 days.

July 26, 1944 First refugee camps for Chamorros are established in Asan and Hågat

July 29, 1944 Marines complete the capture of Orote Peninsula and Fonte Plateau.

July 31, 1944 U.S. Marines capture Hagåtña.

August 8, 1944 Advancing U.S. forces discover the Chigu'an Massacre, where more than 40 Chamorro men who assisted in the Japanese northern fortifications were executed.

August 10, 1944 The last command of the Japanese in Yigo at Mataguac falls, and the U.S. declares the island officially retaken.

November 13, 1944 The Guam Combat Patrol is formed and made up of local hunters, policemen and veterans to search for Japanese stragglers.

December 25, 1944 The first war crimes trial is held by the Guam War Crimes Commission. In total, the Commission tried 51 cases involving 144 persons from 1944 to 1949. The majority of those tried were Japanese, but the accused also included Chamorros who had allegedly assisted the Japanese, primarily as interpreters, during the occupation.

July 21, 1945 The first "Liberation Day" is celebrated on the anniversary of the U.S. reinvasion. Far different than the massive parades of today, the commemoration features a Catholic procession and mass to honor the lives lost in the occupation.

August 6, 1945 The *Enola Gay*, launched from airfields in Tinian, drops the first atomic bomb used in war on Hiroshima. A second bomb is dropped three days later on Nagasaki. More than 100,000 people are killed by the two bombs, not including those who would suffer from the radiation.

August 15, 1945 In a radio broadcast, which was the first public speech by a Japanese emperor, Emperor Hirohito announces the surrender of Japan.

ON THE OPEN SEAS IN SEARCH OF HELP

Dawn was beginning to break when Antonio Cruz announced that he wanted to check the western end of the island for Japanese. He said that at one time he remembered seeing some of them at that end of Dåno', and if they were still there, he would shoot them with the rifle that was handed to us as we were leaving Atåte. The sun was already up when he returned and announced that he did not find any of the enemy.

It was now launching time. With all six of us lending hands, the craft was picked up and carried swiftly to the water. We climbed aboard and with Barcinas at the prow waving a white sheet at the end of a long pole, Cruz steered the craft and four of us paddled wildly. The craft started to make good time on our way to the open ocean. But no sooner had we started than an aircraft, most obviously from an American aircraft carrier nearby, flew over us, inspecting us. After circling us a few times and convinced that we posed no threat to anyone, it flew off.

From where we started out that morning, the eastern end of Dåno', our vision of southern Guam was limited to the Malesso' shoreline and part of the Humåtak shoreline. However, as we moved further west, the island's coastline from Humåtak to as far as the Orote Peninsula had all become visible. And what a sight that greeted us that morning! There were hundreds of ships off the

Hågat coastline. The assault to retake the island was now underway. And for us who suffered much under the Japanese, it was clearly a sight of freedom and deliverance from the inhuman enemy. After the shock of seeing that many ships and the joy of knowing that the Americans had begun their plan to recapture the island from their despicable and deadly enemy, we started paddling again. Only now we were rowing faster, more determined to reach an American ship to ask for help for our people.

We soon reached the narrow opening in the reef, the *Sågua gi Dåno'*,[18] through which Cruz deftly steered the canoe to the open sea. There were a number of ships moving around the invasion fleet, obviously lending protection to that armada from enemy submarines. Cruz steered the canoe toward one that appeared headed toward us. The ship either didn't see us or for some reason it continued to move on. But the one following it apparently saw us and it started to head in our direction. It then stopped and apparently waited for us. It was the destroyer U.S.S. *Wadsworth*, DD-516.

Cruz steered the canoe toward the ship. As we came closer to the vessel, we saw that the entire crew was now on the prow looking at us. It was here that Cruz ordered the rifle to be thrown overboard. As we came closer we saw a ladder, a "Jacob's ladder"[19] I later learned, being thrown down the ship's side. And when the canoe reached the ship, Garrido grabbed the ladder and started to climb.

"Uh-uh, not now," said the armed officer at the top of the ladder. He was pointing his small gun—called a "carbine," I learned later—at Garrido. "What do you guys want?"

His lips trembling, Barcinas was too excited to reply, so he asked me to answer the officer.

"We killed the Japanese guarding us, and we are looking for help

---

18 Bay of *Dåno'*
19 A rope ladder with wooden rungs used to access a ship up the side.

The U.S.S. *Wadsworth*: The destroyer that picked up the six Malesso' volunteers after the massacre at Atåte.

Official U.S. Navy Photograph, from the collections of the Naval History and Heritage Command

from the Americans," I said.

After a few minutes, apparently in consultation with higher authorities in the invasion fleet off Hågat, the officer said we could all climb aboard. We were then frisked. In my pocket was a metal cigarette case, a Japanese war spoil at Atåte. It was confiscated but returned to me a few minutes later. Some of the crew members then started to hand out cigarettes and, a short while later, they even brought us lunch. We were so excited that we hardly touched the food.

After about thirty minutes on the ship's fantail, we were told that we would be transferring to another ship. The destroyer then made a wide, sweeping curve and pointed its bow toward the huge armada outside Hågat where we were met by a flat bowed, flat bottomed craft, a "Higgins boat," I learned was, which was waiting to take us to the large transport vessel, the U.S.S. *George Clymer*, APA-27.

Immediately after we boarded the *Clymer*, we were asked if we knew where the Japanese were on the island. I then told them that barely a week prior I had left Otdot, in the center of the island, where I was forcibly detained for four days. In Otdot there were mounts of munitions all over the place and guarding them were Japanese soldiers.

On the *Clymer*, they then took us to a large room on whose four walls were composite photographs of the entire island: one would have no trouble following the road from Yigo at the northern end of the island to Humåtak at the southern end. I had no problem identifying Otdot. I had hardly finished pointing out the precise location before an officer left the room. I was to learn later that the place was heavily bombed by U.S. carrier planes, resulting in huge explosions doubtlessly from the munitions caches being hit.

Our group broke up after arriving on the *Clymer*. Barcinas and Antonio Cruz, both of whom had left families behind in Atåte, left the ship the next day, followed a day or two later by Juan Cruz, Joaquin

The U.S.S. *George Clymer*, to which the six volunteers from Malesso' were transported from the U.S.S. *Wadsworth* for debriefing.

U. S. Navy photograph

Manalisay, and Juan Garrido. They later said they had looked for me when they were ready to leave, but since the ship had become my bailiwick[20] soon after I stepped on board, they were unable to find me.

The following day, three other men in a different canoe from Malesso' were rescued by the *Clymer*: Jesus Cruz Anderson, Tomas T. Tajalle and Joaquin Cruz Barcinas. All three were active-duty members of the U.S. Navy and were on the Japanese blacklist, but had survived the Tinta massacre.

Our plea for help, first expressed as we boarded the U.S.S. *Wadsworth*, did not fall on deaf ears. But we were told, as we came aboard the *Clymer*, that it was impossible to send a contingent of U.S. soldiers to Atåte (or to wherever the people went after the enemy had been killed) to guard the people against retaliatory effort by the Japanese. Instead, they were sending five soldiers to where the Chamorros went after Atåte to bring them to Hågat where they would be under the protection of the U.S. troops already there.

I was later told that there was a celebratory mood among the people when the five-member U.S. Army team, led by Joaquin Barcinas and his group, reached *Finile*. There was dancing, hugging, kissing and back-slapping after the people realized that the war was over for them and that they had survived. One woman later told me of the American soldiers: "They were so tall, so ruggedly handsome and I hugged and even kissed one of them," she said.

After bringing together the groups that went to *As Båyu* and *Halaohan*, they started the long and arduous trek by the seashore to Hågat since there were no mountain roads then connecting Humåtak with Hågat.

On the *Clymer*, I was berthed in a hold once occupied by combat troops now ashore and fighting the Japanese. It was hot in the hold,

20   Area of interest

but I was there only for sleeping. There was a lot of clothing, shoes and other items that had been discarded by the troops. After almost three years of running around bare-footed and suffering cuts and bruises to my feet, I thought I'd look around and see if I could find a shoe that fit. I did find one that almost fit me if I stuffed the front end with rags. But it was painful and most uncomfortable walking around in stuffed footwear, so I took the shoes off and threw them away.

PUT ASHORE

Four days after I arrived on the *Clymer*, I was put ashore on the Hågat beach in the midst of an Army headquarters detachment. I quickly put up the pup tent they gave me and dug a trench around the tent to keep out the water from the near-incessant rain.

The intense pre-invasion bombardment had damaged or destroyed all the big trees making the Hågat beachhead and the surrounding territory a no man's land. In Atåte, we never heard the cacophony of intense sounds produced by ships offshore cannonading the beachhead. The thick foliage surrounding us had served to deaden the sounds before they reached our ears.

The morning after I was put ashore at the Hågat beach, we were awakened by the sound of intense cannonading by ships. It was still too dark to see the ships, but we could see flashes belching from long, big guns. We learned later the ships were battleships, some of which were badly damaged, sunk, or capsized at Pearl Harbor three years earlier, and now they were firing their sixteen-inch guns at the Orote airfield!

The American invasion plan called for the troops landing at Åsan to swing southwestward to meet with the Hågat assault force moving up from the south. The combined forces would then attack and capture the Japanese airfield on Orote Peninsula.

Amazingly, the devastated Orote airfield was made operational by the U.S. Navy's Construction Battalion or Seabees in two days. Carrier planes would use this base to operate against the Japanese forces who had retreated with their artillery and war tanks to Yigu. The Japanese had planned to battle the Americans there in what was to be their last and desperate stand against them on Guam.

At daybreak, the battleship bombardment of the airfield lifted and planes from off-shore carriers started their intense bombing of the *Orote* airfield. This was followed later by heavy artillery fire erupting behind us. After that, we heard orders for the troops to start moving toward the airfield.

MY PEOPLE ARRIVE AT THE HÅGAT CAMP

It was well after dark on the fourth day since I had been put ashore at the Hågat beachhead when I was awakened from my sleep by noises outside. I quickly got up to investigate and found that it was my people from Malesso'. It was a joyous reunion for all.

I found my family rather quickly among the crowd—my mother, my seven siblings and my elderly and frail grandmother who, by the grace of God, had thus far survived the sheer privations and danger provoked by the inhumane enemy. My fellow villagers all appeared rather well considering what they had gone through.

The military quickly put up a number of large tarpaulin tents to shelter the tired, yet no longer frightened people. The villagers had not eaten for a number of days, and the plentiful military C-rations that were passed out must have assuaged the hunger pains they had been suffering during their days of privations.

THE MALESSO' PEOPLE RETURN HOME

After about four-or-five days in the Hågat camp, the American military command announced that Malesso' village and its surrounding areas were free from the enemy and were safe enough for people to return to their homes. Shortly thereafter, we started the return trek to our homes, long and arduous as it was.

By mid-afternoon, the vanguard of returning Malesso' villagers had reached Humåtak. In the vicinity of the village's church, someone found on the ground a strange-looking contraption on the ground. Initially, no one could identify what it was. Someone suggested it could be a Japanese hand grenade. At this, everyone became frightened and all fled to as far away as possible from the thing. One man stepped forward, held the contraption in his hand and declared that indeed it was a hand grenade. But no one should be frightened, he said, because he knows everything about hand grenades.

And so he stood there examining the contraption, looking at it from top to bottom, and turning it around, all the while declaring that he knew what he was doing. The man then tapped the end of the contraption against a nearby rock and in a matter of seconds, the thing exploded in his hands.

This was the same man who, earlier in our story, claimed that in a fight with another man, his neck was cut with a machete for which the assailant was severely beaten by a Japanese army officer. This was also the man who was in the porter- contingent group carrying ammunition from Malesso' to Otdot when suddenly he dropped to the ground clutching his belly and screaming in pain, convincing the Japanese supervising the portage that his pain was for real and he was released from his labor.

WE REACH OUR *LÅNCHO*

In due time, we reached our *låncho* at *Sumai Malesso'*. In some ways, the place had changed, and in other ways, it appeared like we had not left the place. For one thing, the sleeping mats, pillows and sheets were still on the floor as if the family was preparing to go to bed. But the plantation, a short distance away, was now overgrown with weeds and shrubbery.

A most amazing thing happened in our absence. Before the family left our *låncho* to be herded to Atåte by the Japanese, *Tatan Ben* untethered our female *karabao* so that she could roam wherever and whenever she wanted. Well, there she was, laying under a shady tree chewing her cud and standing next to her was a male, who seemed to be her companion. She even appeared to be pregnant.

Except for the C-rations that the military had given us before we left Hågat, food was scarce, if non-existent. We cleared the plantation for the cultivation of staples we enjoy: taro, *mendioka*, yams, and other root plants. And in these efforts, our female *karabao* friend (we still had not given her a name) seemed to be only too happy pulling the plow as we prepared the field to plant our food.

THE *FÅHA* VICTIMS FOUND

After the Atåte massacre, the effort to find the thirty men who had been selected and led away by the Japanese continued even after the enemies themselves had all been killed. And after the people had returned from Hågat, the search intensified.

It was only then that the same *padre de familia*, who had fed the stray Japanese soldier at the start of our story, admitted seeing the men being herded by the armed enemy up the hill behind the public cemetery. After the *padre* had revealed this information, the search party climbed to the top of the hill and found, sure enough, in a place called Fåha, a shallow trench containing the badly decomposed bodies of the thirty Chamorro males chosen by the murderous enemy because the men were the biggest, strongest, most intelligent and bravest of them all.

A TRIBUTE TO JOSE "POP TONKO" SORIANO REYES

The only male in a sibship of five, *Pop Tonko* was born on March 17, 1920. He and his four sisters—Rosa, Maria, Vicenta and Rita—were the progeny of Jose Ada Reyes and Isabel Meno Soriano. More commonly known by the villagers as *Tun Hosen Esabet*, Tonko's father was a hard-working, kind and deeply religious man possessing a special skill. He sustained his family through hard work on the farm, raising not only foodstuff but poultry, cattle, and pigs; he was a good fisherman as well.

Tun Josen Esabet's farm was located in *Kangan*, some three miles from his home in Malesso'. Every morning, except Sunday when he and his family would all attend Mass, *Tun Jose* would rise before sunup, hitch his *karabao* to the bull cart and take off for the ranch.

Tun Jose's special skill was canoe-making. He would fell a large breadfruit tree and after allowing for the trunk to dry in the sun a few weeks, he would then start hewing to fashion a craft. Someone once said that virtually all canoes in the village were there because of the skill and patience of *Tun Josen Esabet*.

When *Pop Tonko* was old enough, he helped his father by going to the farm after school and performing the chores that his father wanted him to do. His daily trip to the *låncho* became less arduous after his father bought a bicycle for him.

In August of 1939, at age nineteen, *Pop Tonko* married Dolores

Jose "Tonko" Reyes and his wife Dolores.

Courtesy of Jose M. Torres

Leon Guerrero Cruz Lujan, a widow who already had two sons with the late Jose Concepcion Lujan: Jose, born in 1936, and Demetrio, born in 1938. After their marriage, *Pop Tonko* quickly adopted Dolores's sons. In 1939, the couple started having children of their own: John in 1939, Ruth in 1940, Helen in 1941, Elizabeth "Vicky" in 1943, Frankie in 1945, Joseph in 1946, and Kenneth in 1960.

Sometime in the late '30s, *Pop Tonko* sought work with J.H. Pomeroy, the contractor selected to do the island's major fortifications jobs. He was hired on the spot when he demonstrated his proficiency as a heavy equipment operator. This was amazing because *Tonko* did not have experience in operating heavy equipment before he applied for the job with the contractor.

One of the very first jobs J.H. Pomeroy was to perform on Guam was building a breakwater over the reef surrounding outer Apra Harbor. The breakwater was later named the "Glass Breakwater" in honor of Captain Henry Glass, who, as the commanding officer of the battleship U.S.S. *Charleston*, led in the capture of Guam for the Americans on June 20, 1898 shortly after the start of the Spanish-American War.

After he was hired by the contractor, *Pop Tonko* moved his family from Malesso' to Hagåtña and they were there when the Japanese bombed the island on December 8, 1941. He and his family then fled to Malesso' and were there for the remainder of the Japanese occupation.

When the Japanese first occupied the island they quickly issued edicts one after the other. As part of the Work Battalion Six, *Tonko*, along with fifteen-or-twenty other men first grew crops mainly for the Japanese and then later on erected obstacles designed to impede the landing of American war tanks and infantry. When the Japanese began to sow anti-personnel mines designed to kill or maim enemy soldiers attempting to reach dry land, members of the work battalion, but *Tonko* most especially, made mental notes of where they were. One afternoon after the Japanese military had all retreated from the Malesso' area, he started to detonate those mines. He retrieved a Springfield rifle that he had successfully hidden during the war. He then loaded the gun and from a safe distance started shooting at and successfully hitting those detonating arms.

By design or by accident, the Japanese had placed those mines in a strategic location: at the gateway to fertile fishing grounds further out, closer to the reef. Most fishermen would not have been aware that getting to the reef could involve traversing an area mined by the Japanese. But *Tonko* eliminated that danger by successfully setting off all the mines through his sharp-shooting skill.

Pop Tonko had desirable attributes as well. His third oldest son Johnny and Johnny's wife Kathrina remembered him as "soft-spoken, kind, generous and modest."

"Pop was close and loyal to his family members who loved him deeply and would visit him regularly."

Tonko was munificent as well. One of his nephews, Jesus Reyes Garrido, told how shortly after the Reyes clan had returned to *Kangan*, *Pop Tonko* and the others spread out looking for food, which had become acutely scarce. In a few Japanese caches they found some food, mainly rice, which *Tonko* apportioned to the families still living in *Finile* and other nearby areas who had yet to return to their homes in Malesso'.

In the early 1950s, *Pop Tonko* gave a boost to the nascent Guam visitor industry when he started providing daily boat excursions to *Dåno'* and glass-bottom boat and water-skiing services in the *Dåno'* lagoon.

In a press interview shortly after *Pop Tonko's* death, his youngest son Ken was quoted as saying that his father, "was never one of those people who liked a lot of attention. When I was little, I loved to just sit down and hear him talk—if we could get him to talk. I guess he just did what he had to do to stay alive." Ken was referring to his father's leadership in the massacre of the Japanese by the Chamorros at Atåte.

His daughter "Vicky" said that no matter how busy her father was, he always had time to visit his neighbors. "I just called him Mr. Wonderful," she added.

Pop Tonko was not a big man—he stood five feet, six inches tall—but he was especially known for his strength. "When he shook hands, it was like shaking hands with a vise," Ken said. "He was always wanting to arm-wrestle everybody, and he would win."

Over the years, *Pop Tonko* received accolades from the island's leaders. His bravery and leadership were recognized by the 12th and 20th Guam Legislatures. In 1974, the Guam Jaycees named him Grand Marshall for their Fourth of July celebrations, and in 1985 he was honored by the Andersen Air Force Base's Noncommissioned Officer Leadership School for his "acts of heroism and valor."

In all, *Pop Tonko's* family unanimously praised their father for his fine qualities: munificence, loyalty to family and friends, kindness, soft-spoken nature, religious devotion, and physical and moral strength.

On August 18, 2001, *Pop Tonko* died and shortly thereafter the Guam Legislature passed a resolution, "extending the heartfelt condolences of *I Mina'Bente Sais Na Liheslaturan Guahan* to the family of the late Jose Soriano Reyes upon his passing, and to memorializing his outstanding contributions to the people of Guam."

AFTERWORD

"The Uprising at Atåte"

Michael Lujan Bevacqua, Ph.D.
Curator, Guam Museum
Former Assistant Professor of Chamorro Studies, UOG

HÅCHA: Three Massacres

World War II is often referred to as *I Tiempon Chapones* or "The Japanese Time" in Chamorro memory to denote the brutal Japanese colonization of Guam. In July 1944, as this traumatic period was coming to an end and the American reoccupation was on the horizon, three massacres took place near the southern village of Malesso' (later Anglicized as Merizo) at, respectively, Tinta, Fåha and Atåte. During the Tinta and Fåha events, Japanese soldiers forced groups of Chamorros, particularly those who were strong community leaders and icons of resistance, into *bokkongo*[21] and then massacred the Chamorros with gunfire, grenade explosions, and bayonets. The massacre at Atåte, or as I refer to it "The Uprising at Atåte," presented a very different, indeed opposite scenario, as a group of Chamorro men chose to rise up and fight back, killing most of the Japanese soldiers who were holding them captive and threatening their and their families' lives. These Chamorros effectively liberated themselves.

The massacres at Tinta and Fåha are well-established as canonical historical events of *I Tiempon Chapones*. These two famous instances of Chamorro suffering have been deemed significant enough that

---

21   Man-made caves

they are marked with physical monuments, annual memorials, and academic, popular, and media attention. The brutal Japanese massacres of Chamorro people at Tinta and Fåha are common knowledge, included with Magellan's landing, the death of San Vitores, the Spanish-American War, and the U.S. Organic Act, as historical cruxes of significance profound enough to be referents and commonplace knowledge for the average island citizen.

Atåte's massacre bears a very different significance as a record of Chamorro heroism and courage and active resistance. Perhaps foremost because of the very signification of indigenous Chamorro power and resistance to foreign exploitation and occupation, the events at Atåte have never been commemorated with the fervor that drives memorials of the horrific massacres at Tinta and Fåha. There is no physical monument celebrating the Chamorro resistance at Atåte, no plaques for the men who fought heroically with simple tools or their bare hands to save their families, and no annual mass or other memorials. Atåte is a tale largely excluded from canonical history and is known primarily by academics and the descendants of those "mighty men of Merizo."[22] In most Guam history texts it is glossed over as an interesting piece of trivia, but little more.

In this essay, I first place the Uprising at Atåte in its historiographical context to elucidate the evolution of Chamorro identity and the twisting of the narrative of their experiences during *I Tiempon Chapones* and the United States' "liberation" of the island. Chamorro self-conceptualization as a people has shifted rapidly over the past century, in particular Chamorro self-conceptualization in relation to the United States. After suffering under Japanese occupation, Chamorros emerge from the ashes of war with their self-conceptions affected enough to now become patriotic, albeit still colonial, subjects

---

22   "Mighty Men of Merizo Smashed Nip Might," *Guam Daily News*, July 1952.

of the U.S. hegemony.

Next, through the historiography of the Uprising at Atåte, I examine the political and cultural systematic structure that creates the loss and lack of recognition of even an event of such significance. The Uprising at Atåte is marked by erasure from Chamorro narratives of colonial oppression during *I Tiempon Chapones*, while the Japanese massacres at Tinta and Fåha, echoing the mass brutality of the occupiers, are elevated to canonical moments. Tinta and Fåha mirror the hegemonic narrative of U.S. liberation and Chamorro dependency, while the Uprising at Atåte reveals a very different Chamorro self-conceptualization and political narrative of active self-determination and resistance to oppression.

Finally, I discuss. the relationship between the Uprising at Atåte and present-day Chamorro nationalist and decolonial political movements and narratives. My description of the events at Atåte as an "uprising" rather than a "massacre" is deliberate. While Chamorros did massacre the Japanese in Malesso', to refer to this as an uprising is meant not only to illustrate their historical rebellion, but also the importance that the events at Atåte achieve in terms of aiding in decolonizing Chamorro history. As an Uprising, Atåte becomes a point of empowerment in Chamorro history, which stands against a legion of colonial-based narratives that fundamentally disempower Chamorros both historically and up to the present.

HUGUA: The Mighty Men of Merizo

The village of Malesso' occupies a very prominent place in the history of *I Tiempon Chapones* for the Chamorro people. Malesso' represents the massive surge in violence and terror inflicted by the Japanese on the Chamorro people toward the end of World War II, as the Japanese recognized the sunset of their control over Guam and realized the inevitability of their defeat by the U.S. forces.

During the thirty-two months of Japanese occupation, an atmosphere of terror was imposed on the Chamorro people. Chamorro *manåmko'* (elders) who survived *I Tiempon Chapones* recall the period as a constant, difficult, and perilous struggle for survival. Most able-bodied men and women were forced to work daily in fields to produce food for the Japanese, leaving them to find their own food sources during the night. Goods and property of all descriptions, including Chamorro homes, food, and land, were subject to seizure at any time by the Japanese. Chamorros were severely restricted in the language they could use or the materials they could read. Those who were suspected of helping U.S. holdouts hiding on Guam were particularly targeted for arrest, torture or execution. Any Chamorro suspected of resistance was dealt with in the harshest manner. The Japanese military command deliberately and systematically imposed inhumane regulations on Chamorro women, who, regardless of such considerations as age or marital status, were forced to live under the constant threat of conscription into sexual slavery as well as casual rape by Japanese soldiers.

Under such circumstances, most Chamorros strove to evade the notice of their latest colonizers. Many, though by no means all, were fortunate enough to live whole months or years under the Japanese without experiencing any direct personal brutality or trauma. *I Tiempon Chapones* is characterized by violence primarily during the initial attack in December 1941 and then in the final months, both periods when Japan left the island under military control. For the majority of *I Tiempon Chapones*, between those military bookends, a civilian administration called the *Minseibu* was in charge of the island, with a much smaller presence and far less cruel or blatant in their oppression of Chamorros[23].

---

23   Wakako Higuchi, *A US Territory in Japan's Micronesia: The Japanese Navy Administration of Guam, 1941-1944* (Jefferson, NC: McFarland & Company, 2010).

As Japan lost progressively more and more ground during World War II, and U.S. forces took Saipan in June 1944, the actions of the Japanese military command and ordinary soldiers on Guam became more and more undisciplined and violent. The U.S. strategy of gradually moving closer and closer to the Western Pacific and the Marianas in particular during the final half of 1944, eventually pummeling the island of Guam with thirteen days of relentless bombardment, had a part in causing the most severe trauma of the entire war for the Chamorro people. During this period of the inexorable U.S. juggernaut, the Japanese greatly increased murders and executions of Chamorros, including such resistance leaders as *Påle'*[24] Jesus Baza Duenas. The Japanese even executed ordinary Chamorros assisting in the building of Japanese defenses, to keep any small pieces of intelligence they might possess from the U.S. invaders. The majority of Chamorros who had survived the prior events of *I Tiempon Chapones* spent the final weeks of Japanese imperial colonialism being herded into concentration camps at various points on the island, the largest and now-infamous being Mannengon in the island's central valley.

During these final weeks, the Japanese organized and carried out the brutal Tinta and Fåha massacres. The basic details are well known and not in dispute, although there remain countless theories as to the Japanese's motivations. On July 15, 1944, the Japanese called the people of Malesso' together and read aloud the names of thirty of the most influential and powerful of the village's residents. The Japanese falsely declared that these thirty were to be part of a special work detail. The Japanese marched the thirty Chamorros into the swampy area known as Tinta and forced them into a *bokkongo*, where they were told to go to sleep and prepare for work the next day. While it was dark and rainy, and the Chamorros lay unawares,

---

24   Father

the Japanese hurled grenades into the cave to kill as many as possible, before then entering the cave and using bayonets to finish off those who were wounded. Fourteen people survived, however, by using the bodies of those killed to hide themselves.

The next day, on June 16, another thirty names were read publically in Malesso', this time only men, among whom were the strongest of all the members of the village community. They were marched into the hills above the village to an area known as Fåha. Less is known about this massacre because, unlike Tinta, there were no survivors. On this occasion, to ensure that there were no survivors, the Japanese used machine guns in addition to grenades and bayonets to slaughter the Chamorro people marked for such summary execution.

When word reached the rest of the village that these work details were in fact massacres, the people of Malesso' decided to rise up and defend themselves against the senseless butchery. Jose Soriano Reyes, known as Tonko, organized a group of men to protect the lives of the people of Malesso' and resist the Japanese brutality. They conducted their assault in two parts. First, Tonko and a small group of men attacked a supply depot in *As Liyo,* where they killed four Japanese using their fists and stones as well as Tonko's rifle. Second, the Men of Malesso' made their way to Atåte, where the Japanese had imprisoned the majority of the Malesso' people. On the way, Tonko outlined his strategy to his guerrilla force of roughly twenty men. Tonko would hide his rifle while the rest of the ragtag militia would infiltrate the camp, sneaking up on all the Japanese sentries and the tent where some of the Japanese were sleeping. Tonko would give a single shout of command and then everyone would attack at once, in force, to crush their Japanese oppressors before anyone could react. Although there was some hesitation and fear among the Men of Malesso', the plan worked well and they were able to defeat and kill five-of-the-six Japanese soldiers in the camp, with only one

Japanese man escaping to Inalåhan.

After the success of the Uprising at Atåte, the newly liberated Chamorros at Atåte were divided over what to do next. Some were happy to be free from the Japanese and eager to flee to safety, while others were worried about possible retaliation. Led by Jesus Barcinas, six of the Men of Malesso' who had participated in the Uprising at Atåte, led by Jesus Barcinas, found a canoe and navigated northward, hoping to reach the U.S. ships which were circling the island. They succeeded in making friendly contact, first with a suspicious crew from the U.S.S. *Wadsworth*, who were unprepared to communicate with the new-fledged Chamorro liberators waving white flags from their canoes. These representatives of Malesso' were later transferred to the U.S.S. *George Clymer*, where they were debriefed, provided information as to the defensive fortifications of the Japanese on the island, and requested assistance for the people of Malesso'.

TULU: Hafa Esta Matuge'?[25]

In terms of existing Guam History texts, Tinta, Fåha and even Atåte are all commonly noted when discussing this part of *I Tiempon Chapones*. Atåte however is generally given less attention than the massacres at Tinta and Fåha and treated in very interesting historiographical ways considering its content as a historical event.

A Complete History of Guam by Paul Carano and Pedro Sanchez does not mention Tinta, Fåha or Atåte by name but does refer to them. This text has long been noted for being far from complete as it is rigidly focused on the interventions of colonizers and visitors to Guam and does little to tell the Chamorro story of their own island's history. The sections on *I Tiempon Chapones* rarely mention

---

25   *Translation:* What is already written?

a Chamorro name and in truth focus a great deal on describing Chamorro suffering and a longing for the United States to return, but the book does offer one surprise. Unlike the rest of the texts I will discuss, *A Complete History of Guam* provides more textual attention to the Uprising at Atåte than the massacres at Tinta and Fåha. Here is the reference to the massacres:

> In Merizo and Agat, scores of Guamanianas were herded into caves and air-raid shelters and blasted with hand grenades. Some lived to tell of the horrible experience, but most of them died.[26]

Whereas Carano and Sanchez provide the following descriptions for the Uprising at Atåte:

> On July 21, the day American forces landed on Guam, eight men in Merizo hastened their liberation by revolting against their Japanese guards and killing about sixteen of them. The men then paddled their canoes out to sea, where they were picked up by American Naval forces.[27]

Pedro Sanchez would later go on to write several more history books, two of which, *Uncle Sam Please Come Back to Guam* and *Guam: 1941-1945: Wartime Occupation and Liberation* focused exclusively on *I Tiempon Chapones*. *Guahan Guam The History of Our Island* is a comprehensive Guam history text, but features an extensive section on *I Tiempon Chapones*. In these texts Sanchez provides considerable coverage of the massacres at Tinta and Fåha, and also invokes Atåte at interesting narrative points. He gives it great weight, as a discursive

---

26   Paul Carano and Pedro Sanchez, *A Complete History of Guam* (Rutland: Charles Tuttle Company, 1964), 288.
27   Ibid, 292-293.

volta, a piece of historical trivia that helps the overall narrative switch gears. He does this even though his sections on Atåte are always significantly shorter than those on Tinta and Fåha.

In *Guam: 1941-1945: Wartime Occupation and Liberation*, Sanchez provides a paragraph on Atåte. He begins it with "eight men in the village of Merizo hastened their own liberation by revolting against Japanese guards."[28] And after recounting briefly the Uprising at Atåte, he notes, "The liberation of Chamorros had begun."[29] This text is repeated almost verbatim in his later text *Guahan Guam The History of Our Island*.

In another text, *Uncle Sam Please Come Back to Guam*, Sanchez discusses the Uprising at Atåte briefly again, but notes that it was an exceptional act. It was an event that was unique during *I Tiempon Chapones* in terms of characterizing Chamorro resistance or interactions with their occupiers. He writes, "In keeping with their character as a people, the Guamanians eschewed open confrontation with Japanese authorities and avoided violence against the occupation forces."[30] As will be discussed later in this article, this is generally the way Chamorro resistance is articulated during the war, with Chamorros depicted as being primarily passive and quiet in their resistance, choosing not to be open and blatant about it. Atåte doesn't conform to his overall thesis on Chamorro resistance as he notes later:

> There were exceptions, of course. The most notable one was the eight Merizo men who banded together and killed several Japanese guards in their village to stop them from doing any more harm to the residents.[31]

---

28   Pedro C. Sanchez, *Guam: 1941-1945: Wartime Occupation and Liberation* (Tamuning, GU: PC Sanchez Publishing House), 103.
29   Ibid, 104.
30   Pedro C. Sanchez, *Uncle Sam Please Come Back to Guam* (Tamuning, GU: Pacific Island Publishing Company, 1979), 156.
31   Ibid.

Destiny's Landfall by Robert Rogers is the most comprehensive Guam History textbook to date, although Chamorro Studies scholars have nonetheless criticized it for continuing to perpetuate certain colonial narratives.[32] Rogers's mention of the massacres in Malesso' appears towards the end of his chapter on the Japanese occupation. The Uprising at Atåte is reduced to only two sentences, while two full paragraphs are devoted to talking about the massacres at Tinta and Fåha and their subsequent memorialization. One of those sentences follows the example of Sanchez and provides a powerful discursive *volta*, even if the event itself is barely discussed. Rogers writes that Merizo is "the first village on Guam to be liberated, and the only one liberated by Chamorros themselves."[33] Although Rogers focuses little on Atåte itself, he does devote a full paragraph to the acts of Jesus Barcinas and his five compatriots who paddled in canoes out to the American ships seeking aid.

An Island in Agony written by Tony Palomo represents the most complete Chamorro-focused account of *I Tiempon Chapones*. Tony Palomo, like Pedro Sanchez, was a survivor of *I Tiempon Chapones*. He wrote *An Island in Agony* as not only his own testament of what he experienced, but also as a means of telling what he referred to as "the tragic story of the people of Guam, unwitting and helpless pawns in the great Pacific War."[34] Palomo features an extensive account by a survivor of the Tinta Massacre, Manuel Charfauros, something Sanchez also does in order to communicate the horror of the event. Whereas two pages of testimony are devoted to describing the horrors of one of the massacres, only four sentences are used to discuss the Uprising at Atåte. Palomo, in truth, doesn't even use the word

---

32   Robert F. Rogers, *Destiny's Landfall: A History of Guam* (Honolulu: University of Hawaii Press, 1999), 180.
33   Ibid, 181.
34   Tony Palomo, *Island in Agony* (self-pub., Hagatña, GU, 2004) xi.

Atåte. He writes

> When the people of Merizo learned about the massacres, they decided to attack the Japanese, with weapons. In broad daylight, about 20 Merizo men stormed the Japanese quarters seized whatever weapons they could lay their hands on, and killed every Japanese in sight. A hefty Merizo man killed a Japanese soldier with his bare hands. Only one Japanese escaped the wrath of the Merizo people. He managed to flee towards Inarajan, a neighboring village some seven miles to the east.[35]

Palomo, unlike Sanchez, doesn't situate the acts of these Men of Malesso' as a liberation. The term doesn't appear anywhere in the brief discussion of Atåte. He instead focuses on these acts of bravery as being in response to the Japanese massacres. Palomo features a chapter that discusses "Liberation" and recounts the acts of U.S. military men (some of whom were Chamorro) who invaded the island to retake it from the Japanese. But he situates the massacre in his atrocities chapter titled "Bloody Sabers." Like Rogers, Palomo provides more attention to the attempts by the Men of Malesso' to contact the American ships surrounding the island. He provides an entire page, through the account of Jesus Barcinas, covering the details of their paddling out and being picked up by the U.S. Navy.

The website *Guampedia*, as a peer-reviewed online encyclopedia, is an increasingly important source of information for the general public about issues of Guam and Chamorro History. As part of a collection of entries dealing with "War Atrocities" it features an entry on the massacres at Tinta and Fåha. While there is no separate entry for "War Heroism" or "War Resistance," the Tinta and Fåha entry

---

35   Ibid, 187.

features three sentences on the Uprising at Atåte under the heading "Merizo Men Rebel," which reads:

> When the Merizo people learned of the massacres, they were outraged. On July 20, in broad daylight, a group of Merizo men stormed the Japanese quarters at Atåte (another area of the village) and killed ten Japanese soldiers. Only one Japanese soldier escaped, fleeing towards the neighboring village of Inarajan.[36]

The entry ends with a list of those who were victimized at the Tinta and Fåha massacres but does not mention the name of any of the men who fought the Japanese at Atåte.

Don Farrell, a Marianas historian, in his book *A Pictorial History of Guam: Liberation—1944* provides the most extensive coverage of the Atåte massacre. He devotes nine pages to the discussion of the events in Malesso' during the massacre and the uprisings. He doesn't provide the most detailed account of the Uprising at Atåte, but he does situate it in ways that no other text does. All of the mentions covered so far reduce the events at Atåte to two basic moments, the fight against the Japanese in the concentration camp and the paddling out in a canoe to communicate with the American ships. Farrell's narrative goes beyond this, not reducing the heroism of the Men of Malesso' or Chamorros to a single moment, but as part of a longer struggle. He writes:

> Several of the men from Merizo, led by Jose S. Reyes, realized that the Japanese were slaughtering the Chamorros and plotted an uprising. The men overpowered and killed their Japanese guards,

---

36   Leo Babauta, "War Atrocities: Tinta and Fåha Cave Massacres," Guampedia 2009, accessed June 13, 2014, URL: http://guampedia.com/war-atrocities-tinta-and-faha-cave-massacres/.

took their weapons, and continued the fight against the Japanese until Marines finally arrived in the area on July 30, 1944.[37]

Farrell situates the Uprising at Atåte as not a single moment, or even just a hastening to an American liberation, but a real fight, a battle that Chamorros undertook. His reference to Chamorros killing the Japanese, taking their weapons and continuing the fight, communicates the rarely publicized fact that Chamorros did not only fight the Japanese at Atåte, but continued to do so for more than a week afterwards. Farrell reproduces passages in his text from the journal of Jesus Reyes Quinene, a former member of the Guam Militia who along with Jose "Tonko" Soriano Reyes and other men from Malesso' fought and killed dozens of Japanese in the surrounding area before the United States military ever reached them. Farrell, far more than any other writer, gives the Uprising at Atåte a serious political weight, as not just something trivial or an exceptional event that can be brushed aside briefly. He uses terms that no other historian uses in describing the characters of those brave Men of Malesso':

> For the people of Merizo, the incident was one of heroism and valor. In the face of extermination, the Chamorros had fought and saved their families and their honor.[38]

Farrell's representation of the events in Malesso' comes closest in terms of portraying what transpired in Atåte as an uprising. He ascribes to the actions of Chamorros a heavy historical valence, identifying them as heroes in need of recognition and their story in need of retelling. As shown in this section, however, his representation is

---

37   Don Farrell, *The Pictorial History of Guam: Liberation—1944* (Tamuning, GU, Micronesian Productions, 1984), 47.
38   Ibid, 53.

not the norm.

FATFAT: Americans-in-Waiting

I Tiempon Chapones is the most significant event in recent Guam history. It holds the most discursive weight in terms of shaping Chamorro identity today and establishing parameters for Chamorro possibility. Situating the *I Tiempon Chapones* experiences of Chamorros is essential in understanding the way Chamorro identity has shifted over the past eighty years. In everyday island discourse, World War II, or "the war" as it is commonly referred to, can be used to explain everything from the geography of the island (most importantly the military bases), the psychology of the Chamorro people, the high Chamorro levels of service in the U.S. military, and the basis for Chamorros' patriotic self-conceptualization in relation to the U.S. colonial hydra.[39] As if highlighting this importance, the end of the *I Tiempon Chapones* period has been commemorated with the holiday "Liberation Day." This is Guam's largest day of commemoration, where thousands come out to participate in carnivals, parades and beauty pageants.[40]

Michael W. Cruz, a former Lieutenant Governor of Guam and a veteran of the U.S. Army, described the legacy of World War II in 2008 for an interview with *The Washington Post*. In the article, "Guam's Young Steeped in History Line Up to Enlist," he recounted the stories learned from his grandmother and provided his own insight into how we might situate those experiences today:

---

39   Victoria Leon Guerrero, *Of a Tree of People*, Unpublished M.A. Thesis (Mills College, 2008).

40   Vicente M. Diaz, "Deliberating 'Liberation Day': Identity, History, Memory and War in Guam," *Perilous Memories: The Asia Pacific War(s)*, eds., T. Fujitani, Geoffrey M. White and Lisa Yoneyama Eds. (Duke University Press, Durham, NC: Duke University Press, 2001).

Cruz's grandmother told him awful stories: She was held in a concentration camp. She was forced to watch as Japanese soldiers chopped off the heads of her brother and her eldest son. Her eldest daughters were forced into prostitution.
[According to Cruz:] 'We saw war in color—the beaches were splattered with blood . . . if there is a group of Americans who understand the price of freedom, we do.'[41]

This type of statement is commonplace among Chamorros today, situating Chamorro identity within not only a generic American, but an extremely patriotic American context. Thus, the Chamorro as a subject today is not just any political subject, but one inundated with a supposed secret knowledge of the U.S. and its potential, and therefore is first and foremost a deeply obeisant patriotic vassal of the U.S. *patria*.[42] This sort of statement, however, would have been almost unheard of prior to *I Tiempon Chapones* and the U.S. re-invasion and re-colonization of Guam. Since 1898, Guam has been a colony of the United States, however the U.S. return and "liberation" in 1944 represents a watershed moment where the colonial relationship itself does not change, but the way Chamorros perceive it does.

Prior to the war, Chamorros saw themselves as culturally and politically a distinct entity from the United States, although technically under its rule. They did not overtly challenge the authority of the United States, but did not outwardly express loyalty either. Pre-*Tiempon Chapones*, efforts by the United States to instill a sense

---

41   Blaine Harden, "Guam's Young, Steeped in History, Line Up to Enlist," *The Washington Post*, January 27, 2008.
42   Michael Lujan Bevacqua, "Laboratory of Liberation and Non-Voting Delegates," in *Ghosts, Chamorros and Non-Voting Delegates: GUAM! Where the Production of America's Sovereignty Begins!*, PhD diss. (University of California, San Diego, 2010).

of internalized colonial attitudes and patriotism in Chamorros had only limited success, in particular among the Chamorro elite.[43] As I will discuss later in this article, Chamorros felt their difference to the United States strongly, not only through the colonial discrimination and racialization imposed by the U.S., but also through a surviving shred of sovereignty that allowed discursive space for awareness of alterity, even after different nations had sought to impose colonial narratives on their lands and lives.

In his article "Teaching Guam's History in Guam High Schools," Chamorro scholar, politician, and decolonization activist Robert Underwood makes this point clear: "The Chamorro people were not Americans, did not see themselves as American-in-waiting, and probably did not care much about being American."[44] *I Tiempon Chapones* marked a turning point in this Chamorro self-conceptualization. Chamorros prior to the war did not imagine themselves to be a part of the United States, as Underwood states, but also, after the war, they suddenly seemed unable to imagine themselves as anything but devoted to it. In the ashes of *I Tiempon Chapones*, Chamorros saw the future in red, white, and blue and could not conceive of any other possibility. As Francisco Baza Leon Guerrero, a Chamorro civil rights pioneer, was infamously known to say after the war, "The only '-ism' on Guam is Americanism."[45]

The Japanese had accomplished in thirty-two intense months what the U.S. had failed to do across forty-one uneven and inconsistent

---

43 Penelope Bordallo Hofschneider, *Campaign for Political Rights on the Island of Guam, 1898-1950*. (Saipan: CNMI Division of Historic Preservation, Saipan, Commonwealth of the Northern Marianas Islands, 2001).

44 Robert Underwood, "Teaching Guam's History in Guam High Schools," in *Guam History Perspectives,* eds., Lee Carter, Rosa Carter, and William Wuerch (Mangilao: University of Guam, Guam, 1997), 7.

45 Robert Underwood, *Interview With Author*, National Pacific Island Education Network, California Sate University Long Beach, Long Beach, California, 15 November 2003.

years of colonization and indoctrination: the Japanese brutality fired the ascension of excessive Chamorro patriotism for the United States. *I Tiempon Chapones* is the event that, despite Guam's unchanged colonial status, has given Chamorro self-conceptualization in relation to the United States its current enthusiastic, internalized character. This relationship, however, is irreducible to simple patriotism and cannot be described in terms of mindless sycophancy. Just as Chamorros evince intense patriotism to the United States today, they also regularly recognize a certain disrespect present in the relationship, as if "Uncle Spam" is not properly recognizing them and is not giving them their deserved dignity.

LIMA: The Scene of Liberation

In order to explain further this U.S. colonization of not only Chamorro land but also Chamorro self-conception, I shall refer to my previous work describing what I call the Scene of Liberation.[46] Amidst all the possible memories and moments that could represent *I Tiempon Chapones* in the popular imagination and hegemonic political narratives, there is one particular moment, one certain Scene of Liberation, which has come to signify the potential political meanings associated with this historic event. This moment appears in newspaper and magazine advertisements for banks, grocery stores, and political candidates and is commemorated regularly throughout the year on overtly militarized and patriotic holidays such as "Liberation Day," "Veterans' Day," "Memorial Day," and "Independence Day" or the Fourth of July. This Scene of Liberation is invoked in an everyday sense also to articulate a number of political points, whether it be

---

46   Michael Lujan Bevacqua, *The Scene of Liberation*, Unpublished Paper Presented at the First Marianas History Conference, Saipan, CNMI, 2012.

an explanation for a Chamorro's personal patriotism to the United States, expressions of Guam's dependency on the U.S. or the need for a greater U.S. military presence on the island.[47]

This event is what I call the Scene of Liberation, the moment when the Japanese occupation that had traumatized Chamorros for thirty-two months at last came to an end. It is often reduced to an archetypical image, a scene in which destitute Chamorros meet young U.S. Marines. The Chamorro feminist scholar Laura Torres Souder, in her article "Psyche Under Siege," provides a very complete yet succinct account of this significant moment, drawing out not only the historical components but the political dimensions as well:

> Drenched by heavy rains, up to their ankles in mud, heads bowed low, spirits sagging, the Chamorros at Mannengon, Maimai, Tai, Talofofo, and Inarajan were desperately clinging to a last ray of hope. In the silence of the night, Pete Rosario began to sing several lines of a song he had composed – 'Sam, Sam, my dear Uncle Sam, won't you please come back to Guam.' It was 1944, the Japanese Imperial Forces had occupied Guam for nearly three years. The brutalities and atrocities of a cruel war on an innocent people had taken their toll…The Japanese herded Chamorros in long arduous marches into concentration camps. Many died. Exhausted, vulnerable, weakened by malnourishment and disease, the Chamorros waited like sheep.
>
> Prayers were answered in that rain-soaked month of July with the second coming of dear old Uncle Sam. Sam came back with thousands of troops to reclaim 'our land' for democracy. The joys of 'liberation' were sweet. Chamorro survivors of World War II

---

47   Michael Lujan Bevacqua, "World War II: Is it Over?" Panel Sponsored by the Guam Humanities Council. Hagatña Shopping Center, Hagatña, Guam, 15 July 2004.

embraced all that was American with overwhelming gratitude and profound respect. Uncle Sam and his men were worshipped as heroes, and rightfully so. No-one who lived through the tyranny of the Japanese occupation went unscathed. Survival became synonymous with American Military Forces.

...Uncle Sam brought freedom from the Japanese. Yes, he brought food to the hungry: K-rations like spam, corned beef, cheese, pork and beans, bacon, powdered eggs, and powdered milk – some of which have become island staples. Yes, he brought medicines to the sick and rebuilt the hospitals and clinics to minister to the health needs of the people. Yes, he brought clothes to the needy through the American Red Cross, a welcome relief to most whose only wardrobe consisted of the clothing on their backs. Yes, he provided shelter to the homeless, first pup tents and Quonset housing, and then wooden houses with tin roofs. Yes, he built schools and provided jobs.[48]

In this description, Souder creates a scene that is in actuality multiple levels of experiences merged together, potent in not simply emotional or historical meaning but political significance as well. For those who lived through this moment, she argues, it was not only an experience of responding emotionally with relief to the brutal decimation of the Japanese colonizer by the U.S. colonizer and its soldiers. Chamorros also felt indebted to the U.S. colonizer in response to the traumatic events of *I Tiempon Chapones*, especially the heightened trauma just before the re-invasion of the United States, and began to equate its return with concepts such as security, safety and

---

48   Laura Torres Souder, "Psyche Under Siege: Uncle Sam, Look What You've Done to Us." *Sustainable Development or Malignant Growth?* (Suva, Fiji Marama Publications, 1994), 193-194.

prosperity. When I refer to this moment as the Scene of Liberation, I am referring not to the literal instance, but rather to the way in which this collage of moments achieves a certain hegemonic character in self-conceptualization and in its reification and commemoration displaces the actual history it claims to (re)present with reality. The Scene of Liberation reduces history to a series of elements that draw people into this narrative, even if those people didn't experience the events of *I Tiempon Chapones* and the U.S. re-invasion and re-colonization themselves. The Scene of Liberation remains hegemonic in the sense that it plays a central role in structuring meaning for subjects that are attached to it. As such, it is always something that you are required to return to and you are unconsciously compelled to articulate your identity in relation to that scene.[49]

The Scene of Liberation reduces history to two basic subject positions. There is the Chamorro, the passive victim of war, destitute, barely subject, who can do nothing else but wait for sustenance, wait for salvation. Towering above this Chamorro is the United States marine, the soldier, the liberator. He beams with power, with prowess, with authority and agency. His uniform is covered not just in sand, mud, and blood, but also stained with glorious ideals like freedom and democracy. He brings to Chamorros so much that is not just appreciated, but by the rules of the event itself, is *necessary*. As Souder notes, the invading marine does not just bring with him the tools that make life possible, but as the soldier, the military, represents survival, and he brings with him life itself. According to the Scene, the Chamorro is made to feel as if life could not be possible without the U.S. figure present.

The Scene is essential in understanding how Chamorros have come to see their own historical and contemporary political

---

[49] Bevacqua, *Scene of Liberation*.

limitations. The previous detachment from the United States largely evaporated, as they were confronted by a new world in which their very existence appeared to be linked to U.S. interventions and liberation. Feelings of patriotism, gratitude, and indebtedness can be expected, as long as these feelings are the kind that do not liberate the Chamorro subjectivity but ensnare it in a new field of dependency.

While Japanese colonial brutality allowed Chamorros to develop feelings of patriotism towards the replacement colonizer of the United States, these feelings were and are based on a fundamentally unequal relationship, where the Chamorro lies in poverty, starving, war-scarred, and the U.S. marine looms overhead holding the keys to Chamorro salvation and prosperity. This patriotism is tinged with subordination because of the debt they owe to the United States for their lives and the lives of their families, which is designed by its nature to be felt as an eternal debt that can never be repaid.

The Chamorro as a U.S. subject born into this scene of liberation is always a minor subject, a subordinated one, who will see inclusion into the United States as requiring him or her to identify with their suffering Chamorro *saina* in Mannengon. This scene does not seem to allow for Chamorros to conceive of themselves as acting in ways that encourage a sense of equality or their own agency.

GUNUM: I Mesgnon-ta[50]

In the wider historiography of *I Tiempon Chapones*, we can also see this dynamic. The Chamorro war experience, as one might expect, is filled with suffering and tragedy. Chamorros are starved, they are beaten, they are raped. They are tortured, and in addition to Tinta and Fåha, other massacres take place. Chamorros are victimized and

---

50   *Translation:* Our endurance.

have little means to fight back.

This narrative of victimization, however, does not stimulate feelings of shame or embarrassment amongst war survivors. While suffering does inundate war narratives, there are also many invocations of toughness, of bravery, of ingenuity in survival. Although Chamorros did not generally violently challenge Japanese oppression, their nonviolent endurance nonetheless allows for self-conceptualization involving courage and triumph, as if the Chamorro people were put to life's most difficult test and survived. The Japanese came to conquer the Chamorros and only succeeded in taking their lands: they could not conquer the Chamorro spirit.

Former Guam Senator Frank Blas Jr., articulated this very well in a column he wrote in the *Marianas Variety* titled "Strength to Go On." During his time in the Legislature, Blas undertook several projects to recognize the stories of Chamorros who survived World War II and regularly referred to them as Guam's "greatest generation."[51] In his column, he writes:

> When faced with swords and bayonets during the war, and later American bombs and bulldozers, the Chamorro people did not lay down to die. They did not give up or give in. They held tightly to their families, their culture, and their unconquerable souls. I imagine an island of 22,000 people—mothers, fathers, children, elders, each reaching deep within themselves to find that strength to go on, to endure and live another day. I can imagine each in their own way, whispering to themselves, 'Estegue i taiå'ñao na ante-ku, ya put este, Guahu i ma'gas i lina'la-hu.'[52]

---

51 Frank Blas Jr., "Remembering Our Greatest Generation," *The Marianas Variety*, December 14 2010.

52 Frank Blas Jr. "Strength to Go On," *The Marianas Variety*, November 23 2010.

Chamorros articulate this idea of Chamorro strength and survival during *I Tiempon Chapones* as a form of resistance, albeit a muted and passive one. In Chamorro, this endurance is often referred to as *"mesngon"* or *"minesngon."* *Mesngon* translates as "durable, able to endure, lasting, enduring, not wearing out"; *minesngon* translates as "durability" or "endurance."[53] The etymological root for both is *"sungon,"* which translates as "to tolerate, endure, sustain, bear, tolerate with patience, withstand, last, to be strong enough."[54]

Minesngon can be and usually is considered to be a value of Chamorros, a rhetorical move that is used to mark their existence in a complicated but nonetheless positive light.[55] This is a stubborn durability indeed. *Minesngon* emblematizes the Chamorro experience during the long historical sequence of colonizers—Spain, the U.S., Japan and the U.S. again, Chamorros have long retained a shred of sovereignty and developed a pride in their durability and toughness. They conceive of themselves as being able to handle whatever the world throws at them.

Minesngon is most commonly expressed through axioms, sayings passed down over time to express the Chamorro relation to the changing of flags over their island and their capacity to adapt effectively. Historian and genealogist Anthony Ramirez notes that this worldview was very common with the generation of Chamorros who saw the changing of the colonial guard three times over in their lives. From them, he heard this saying:

Fanatahguiyan i ha'åni siha

---

53   Donald Topping, Pedro Ogo, and Bernadita Dungca *Chamorro-English Dictionary*. (Honolulu: University of Hawai'i, 1975).
54   Ibid.
55   Vince Bernad Manibusan, *Exploring Low Suicide Rates Through the Wisdom of Chamoru Elders*, Unpublished M.A. Thesis (University of Guam, 2011), 33-34.

Chumåchalek hao på'go
Kumåkasao hao agupa'[56]

This saying tells Chamorros not to be too attached to the world around them, because the political context can change quickly, unexpectedly and seemingly uncontrollably. One will be laughing one day and crying the next. Do not salute too seriously the flag of one master, because any day it may be replaced by that of another. In this context, the Chamorro capacity to adapt and to survive means that they will endure regardless of who claims their island. This is evidenced by another Chamorro phrase, "*I mesngon i manggåna'*!" or "the one who suffers is the one who wins in the end."[57] Thus, the one who patiently endures is the one who will actually triumph.

Chamorro resistance during World War II is not generally characterized by a capacity to lead, to speak out, to demand, or to take charge, but rather a capacity to suffer and be hurt while still standing strong, being brave and not giving in completely. Chamorros can rightfully take pride in such strength under horrific Japanese occupation. However, in terms of historiography, the narrative of *minesngon* can lead to the reduction of the power and significance of divergent Chamorro experiences.

FITI: Resistance the Chamorro Way

If we consider Chamorros in the context of *minesngon* within the narratives surrounding *I Tiempon Chapones*, then it is natural not to see them as the primary actors of this tale, for that role has been assigned to the United States. The United States military can be and generally

---

56   Toni Ramirez, *Interview With Author*, Ordot, Guam, October 11 2000.
57   Laura Torres Souder, *Daughters of the Island: Contemporary Chamorro Women Organizers* (Mangilao: Micronesian Area Research Center, University of Guam, Mangilao, Guam, 1987).

is conceived of as the prime mover, the ultimate decider of fate, like a *deus ex machina*[58] that intervenes to restore order and give the narrative final meaning. The U.S., monolithically conceived, is the sole actor, without which nothing else is possible, as if without the U.S. hegemony the telling of the story is pointless, and the courage and strength of Chamorros is nonexistent.

The *minesngon* discourse further splits into micro-narratives, all of which hinge upon the umbrella narrative of U.S. military might and the propensity of the United States to fight for freedom, to liberate and to save. In narrative terms, Chamorro resistance is admirable, but does not directly challenge the Japanese oppressor and therefore requires someone or something else to intervene and offer salvation. That intervening force of the United States carries the fulfilling agency, the re-invasion and re-occupation that makes Chamorro resistance move from being pointless or *taisetbe*[59] to becoming powerful and beautiful.

We can see this historiographical reduction in the way in which Chamorro actions of resistance become too intimately tied not to strategies for survival, but rather expressions of patriotism towards the United States. The previously mentioned Guam history texts by the late Dr. Pedro Sanchez dealing with *I Tiempon Chapones* exemplify this dynamic. In *Uncle Sam Please Come Back to Guam* he discusses the topic of "Resistance the Chamorro Way" or the particular ways in which Chamorros fought back against the oppression they faced at the hands of the Japanese:

> By and large, resistance during the occupation took on Chamorro flavor. It was not dramatic because the islanders were not given to dramatics. It was not resistance by shooting down invaders and occupation troops, or blowing up bridges and enemy facilities.

---

58   An unexpected power saving a seemingly hopeless situation
59   Worthless

It was a different kind of resistance because it was resistance through and of the spirit.[60]

In talking about these "spirited" and "Chamorro-flavored" acts, song carries high discursive significance for Sanchez as to what exactly constitutes "resistance" in the context of *I Tiempon Chapones*. He discusses the ways Chamorros used the language barrier, the fact that the agents of the Japanese colonizer could not understand Chamorro, as a screen through which the Chamorro people could express themselves and their dislike for their Japanese oppressors while avoiding retaliation.

Take for example "*Ilek-ña Si Sensei*" or "[the Japanese] Teacher Says." Under Japanese colonization, Chamorro children would often be forced to sing to entertain troops.[61] "*Ilek-ña i Sensei*" was sung to the tune of the Christian nativity hymn "O Come, All Ye Faithful" and sounded cheerful and harmless, but was often filled with messages that were critical of the Japanese and supportive of the United States, masked by use of the Chamorro language.

Ilek-ña i Sensei
Na Guiya Yu'us måmi
Lao mandagi i Sensei
Sa' batchigo'
Dami Danaika
Siempre u ma tulaika
I misu yan i kechup
Put i pan yan mantekiya

---

60 Sanchez, Uncle Sam, 156.
61 Cecilia Taitano Perez, "A Chamorro Re-telling of 'Liberation,'" in *Kinalamten Pulitikat: Sinenten I Chamorro: Issues in Guam's Political Development: The Chamorro Perspective* (Agana, Guam: Political Status Education Coordinating Commission, 1996), 72.

Afterword | 137

Ga'na-ku i Amerikånu
Ki Chapones[62]

In this song, Chamorros criticize the Japanese for acting as if they are the new masters not just of Guam, but also over its people. In most versions the song is entirely in Chamorro save for *"dami danaka"* which means "don't lie," admonishing the Japanese for acting like the new deities for Chamorros. The song ends with Chamorros pining for a change in food on the island, eagerly anticipating the day when the Asian foods that have been forced onto their dinner tables will be replaced with American food instead. The last two lines make clear the preference by stating outright, "I prefer the Americans to the Japanese."

The centerpiece however in stitching together Sanchez's argument on Chamorro resistance is the song "Sam, Sam, My Dear Uncle Sam," a song created by Chamorros during *I Tiempon Chapones* in order to express their desire for a return of the U.S. to the island. Chamorros could be punished for singing this song, in part because of its pro-U.S. content but also because of the fact that, in contrast to other resistance songs that were in Chamorro, this one was almost entirely in English.[63]

> Uncle Sam, I'm sad and lonely
> Uncle Sam, come back to me
> Uncle Sam, I love you only
> Oh, please come back and set me free

---

62   *Translation:* The teacher says/ That he is our God/ But teacher is lying/ Because he's cross-eyed/ Don't you believe it!/ Surely it will change/ The miso for the ketchup/ And the bread and butter/ I prefer the Americans/ Instead of the Japanese.

63   See Chapter 4, Michael Lujan Bevacqua, *These May or May Not Be Americans: The Patriotic Myth and Hijacking of Chamorro History on Guam*, M.A. Thesis (University of Guam, 2004).

Early Monday morning
The action came to Guam
Eighth of December
Nineteen forty-one

Oh Mr. Sam, Sam, my dear Uncle Sam
Won't you please come back to Guam?

Our lives are in danger
You better come
And kill all the Japanese
Right here on Guam

Oh Mr. Sam, Sam, my dear Uncle Sam
Won't you please come back to Guam?[64]

Sanchez articulates Chamorro resistance through the playful and lyrical capacities of Chamorros, their ability to sing of their struggles and finding strength to go on in those minor and generally passive acts of defiance. However, Sanchez's descriptions are filled with acts that are ultimately expressions of a newborn loyalty to the U.S. (re)colonizer, not of Chamorro strength per se. These songs acted as a way for Chamorros to vote in their secret hearts, or in whatever small ways they could, for an end to Japanese domination. In terms of articulation, Chamorro resistance thus becomes problematic. The motivations for Chamorros shift from protecting themselves, their families, their culture and their island, to risking their lives in order to express their desire for an American return: they become acts not of resistance, but of loyalty or devotion. The songs express preference

---

64   Sanchez, *Uncle Sam*, 159-160.

for one colonizer over another. Any Chamorro agency moves from being calculating, strategizing, active, and conscious, to a passive one, which is inundated with a wish for the return of a more benevolent colonizer.

In her article "A Chamorro Re-Telling of Liberation," Chamorro poet Cecelia Perez provides a quote from the late Jeff Barcinas, who was from the village of Malesso'. In response to a question about whether the Chamorro experience is given enough weight in the dominant narratives of *I Tiempon Chapones*, Barcinas takes a position in line with what I have written thus far. According to Barcinas, without the United States, "we [the Chamorro people] could have been completely wiped out and we could have been nobody in terms of identity of a people who are seeking right now self-determination."[65]

For Barcinas and for many others, the Chamorro and the Chamorro story are insufficient on their own. The Chamorro in history requires the United States for salvation, and in retelling that story, the Chamorro requires the United States to make the tale complete. All of that which the Chamorro critiques and challenges after the fact must still adhere to the fact that the very existence of the Chamorro, whether as something that critiques or glorifies the United States, required and requires U.S. intervention for existence. Without the United States, the Chamorro story is one of annihilation and impossibility. The Chamorro style of resistance does not liberate in this context, even if it does persevere.

The Chamorro experience in that moment is difficult to discern because of the way Chamorros' everyday actions become situated within a post-bellum teleological continuum as if they were struggling not to protect themselves and their families but to express their loyalty and their devotion to the U.S., something which the

---

65   Perez, "A Chamorro Re-telling," 76.

U.S. repaid in its return to Guam, leading to the Chamorro patriotic matrix discussed earlier.

GUALO: A Heart-Shaped Flag

Tinta and Fåha both fit perfectly within this nexus of Chamorro war experiences defined in terms of suffering and establishing a connection to the United States. The massacres underscore the horrifying nature of Japanese colonialism. Chamorros huddled into *bokkongo* are brave and resolute as they face and accept their fates rather than place their families at risk. They do not act, violently or otherwise, to save themselves and end Japanese oppression. In the end, this is a tragic tale that seems to make clear the desperate nature of Chamorros during *I Tiempon Chapones* and their ardent wishes for a U.S. return.

In addition to the killing that took place, there were American dimensions to these two massacres that helped push the Chamorro towards a subordinate but patriotic relationship to the United States. Although some of those selected by the Japanese to be massacred were chosen because of their previous actions of resistance or their size and physical capability of fighting back should the Japanese attempt to decimate the entire village, some of the victims were chosen because of perceived attachments to the United States.

Some of the victims had sons who were in the U.S. Navy. Some of them had formerly served in the U.S. Navy. Some of them had made known their preference for the U.S. over Japan. The Japanese naturally understood that the Chamorro people resented their colonial subjugation, but still considered it sacrilege for Chamorros to speak of the U.S. aloud. One woman infamously had rejected Japanese rule by refusing to bow to the Japanese in Malesso'.[66] They were

---

66   Farrell, 44.

targeted because of their love for the United States, specifically. These incipient forms of patriotism marked them for execution. These Chamorro people sacrificed and suffered for the United States, and so it is perhaps only natural then that the Chamorro story be one of pining for a U.S. return.

This Americanization of Chamorro experiences under colonialist Japanese brutality centers the replacement colonizer in the Chamorro war story. Even if it was Chamorros who endured *I Tiempon Chapones*, their desire for a U.S. return and salvation subordinates their experiences to a narrative focused on the United States and its re-invasion, re-occupation and liberation of the island.

SIGUA: Searching for Symbols

This colonialized, Americanized narrative of history and the subordinate position it enforces on the Chamorro people can explain much about why Atåte might remain a fragment of history unintelligible or difficult to integrate into canonical Chamorro history. The actions of the Men from Malesso' during the Uprising at Atåte show Chamorros acting in a way that is vastly different from their typical war-time representations. In the Uprising at Atåte, Chamorros exhibited a level of agency that has the potential to disrupt the discursive dynamics I have described thus far.

With the Uprising at Atåte, history must recognize a group of Chamorro men, barely armed, most never trained to fight, much less kill, and scared to death, who nonetheless challenge the might of their colonizer impressed upon them over a period of brutal years. On that day, in that moment, in this new "Scene of Liberation," they defeat the Japanese, terrorize them, and effectively liberate themselves.

Atåte is an unusually uplifting story in the context of the current received history of *I Tiempon Chapones*, and a story rich in what makes any story compelling, something to be passed on, something to be transmitted from one generation to the next. On these merits alone, the Uprising at Atåte and the actions of the Men of Malesso' should be an event of great historical consequence, in which Chamorros could and should take pride. Just as the Chamorro people find virtue in their sacrifices and suffering in the war, this act to save themselves should receive similar levels of cultural honor and respect. In the historical record of the Uprising at Atåte, Chamorros are not passive heroes, but active ones.

Robert Underwood's article, "Red, Whitewash and Blue: Painting Over the Chamorro Experience" functions as the key theoretical point through which the Chamorro war experience has been critiqued and interrogated since the 1970s.[67] His questions and answers are similar to those presented and discussed thus far in this article. The manner in which Liberation Day appears to function in Chamorro culture is as a celebration of overabundant U.S. patriotism with iconic symbols of U.S. power and glory littering the discursive and actual scene. The Chamorro story is erased through this overemphasis on the U.S. The Chamorro experience becomes an effect of or dependent upon U.S. dominance, becoming another hegemonic colonialist narrative. Therefore, a commemorative event such as Liberation Day appears to continue that tendency and obscure the Chamorro to privilege sometimes excessive expressions of patriotic devotion to the United States.

Underwood challenges this assumption, however, by arguing that, even if on the surface it appears that Chamorros are celebrating the United States and appearing to almost erase themselves from their commemoration, this is not the case. Although they are waving United States flags and speaking admiringly of the United States,

---

67   Robert Underwood, "Red, Whitewash and Blue: Painting over the Chamorro Experience," *Pacific Daily News*, July 17 1977, 6-8

they are in truth celebrating themselves. Although Chamorros use U.S. trappings for their commemorations, it is Chamorro sacrifices and the Chamorro story that they are truly remembering.[68]

The Uprising at Atåte and the Men of Malesso' have been scarcely recognized in the historical record, as well as the popular mind: Chamorros have historically ignored the significance of that event as a referent of cultural celebration, let alone liberation from the Japanese. Underwood offers a further helpful insight into this erasure in his article, arguing that the patriotic displays of Chamorro self-celebration are a result of the lack of alternative available commemorative symbols. In the aftermath of the war, as Chamorros were searching for a way to represent their story, their survival, their place in history, the Chamorro as a political subject seemed devoid of possible indigenous symbols.[69] In *I Tiempon Chapones*, the Chamorro is marked by the American red, white, and blue, and the red rising sun of the Japanese. What Chamorro symbol could match, could represent a distinctive Chamorro agency amidst these massive empires of steel clashing around them? As the U.S. flag had come to be so intimately associated with freedom and hope, what could the Chamorro offer the world that could stand beside it? What could they offer that could match the incredible potency of those symbols that, some said, had made the world safe for democracy again?

MANO'FULU: Chamorro Sovereignty

As Chamorros have been under colonial rule for more than three centuries, their feelings of sovereignty have been diffused. Their sense of their existence as a people has shifted dramatically, even, at some

---

68   Ibid, 7.
69   Ibid.

points, appearing to dissipate. Sovereignty is not only a concept of political recognition between nation-states, it is also commonly used in terms of describing the desires and the realities of indigenous people around the world.[70] For many native peoples, it is a mark of continuity in the midst of a history of tragic adversity. Sovereignty offers an empowered feeling of self-identity, even if history seems determined to take away who you are or convince you that you have become something else. In this way, sovereignty is sometimes referred to as nationalism or native nationalism.[71]

The identity of Chamorros has changed over the centuries and this continuity, this sense of distinct peoplehood, can be difficult to discern and trace at times. Chamorro identity at the start of the Spanish period of colonization was very different than at the end, but in both times Chamorros nonetheless saw themselves as a distinct people in the world. With the shifts in Chamorro identity over the centuries, there are also numerous shifts in their consciousness, where you can perceive a nationalist dimension to their existence.

Chamorro nationalism was a vibrant force during the Chamorro-Spanish Wars as most Chamorros actively or passively resisted Spanish attempts to convert and colonize them.[72] Carlos Madrid shows native Chamorro nationalism evolving in a new anti-colonial context, similar to what appeared in the nineteenth century in the Philippines and Puerto Rico, as the Spanish Empire was

---

70   Taiaiake Alfred, *Peace, Power and Righteousness; An Indigenous Manifesto* (Don Mills, Ontario: Oxford University Press, 1999).
Haunani Kay-Trask, *From a Native Daughter: Colonialism and Sovereignty in Hawai'i* (Honolulu, Hawai'i: University of Hawai'i Press, 1999).
Joanne Barkerm ed., *Sovereignty Matters: Locations of Contestation and Possibility in Indigenous Struggles for Self-Determination* (Lincoln: University of Nebraska, 2005).
71   Ronald Niezen, *The Origins of Indigenism: Human Rights and the Politics of Identity* (Berkeley: University of California Press, 2003).
72   Ed Benavente, *I Manmañaina-ta: I Manmaga'låhi yan I Manmå'gas; Geran Chamoru yan Españot (1668-1695)* (Mangilao, Guam: Self-Published, 2007).

dissolving.[73] In the late twentieth century, Chamorro nationalism becomes even more explicit through the formation of groups such as the Organization of People for Indigenous Rights (OPI-R) and Nasion Chamoru. These groups advocated for the Chamorro as a native political subject with rights to certain choices, certain forms of existence, of which colonization had long deprived the Chamorro.[74]

Despite these sporadic spikes in political consciousness, for much of the last 350 years of Guam history, the sovereignty that Chamorros feel is hardly political. Part of every colonial process is the development of binaries through which generally the colonizer is elevated and the colonized is degraded. Through this, the colonized becomes uneducated, dirty, poor and stuck, while the colonizer is meant to appear enlightened, rich, clean and mobile.[75] Chamorros through most of this period have come to conceive of themselves in terms of cultural sovereignty. This extended into the way they envisioned their sovereignty, as deriving not from their political dimensions, but their cultural ones. This sense of sovereignty was heavily supported by the evolution and continued use of the Chamorro language, as it became a marker of Chamorro difference even as it was influenced by outsiders.

This cultural sovereignty did not promote much in terms of active political resistance. It was not the type of sovereignty that would lead to violence or organized collectives for revolution. It was ideal for a passive resistance, and this is the type that characterized most Chamorro interactions with their colonizers. During the Spanish era,

---

73 Carlos Madrid, *Beyond Distances: Governance, Politics and Deportation in the Mariana Islands from 1870 to 1877* (Saipan, CNMI: Northern Mariana Islands Council for Humanities, 2006).

74 Michael P. Perez, "Contested Sites: Pacific Resistance in Guam to U.S. Empire," *Amerasia Journal,* (27:1), 2001, 97-115.

75 Michael Lujan Bevacqua, *Everything You Wanted to Know About Guam But Were Afraid to Ask Zizek,* M.A. Thesis (University of California, San Diego, 2007).

stories of Juan Måla, a fictional folk hero who did not actually fight the Spanish, but rather deceived them and made them appear foolish, animated this feeling of difference, this passive resistance.[76] The Chamorro use of education in the first U.S. colonial era pre-*Tiempon Chapones* and their overall resistance to the eradication of their language were also passive ways of engaging with the colonizer, while still seeing themselves as distinct and not fully accounted for by the colonizing gaze.[77]

Despite the rhetorical and corporeal attempts by different colonizers to absorb Chamorros, the Chamorro people continued to perceive themselves as being fundamentally different. They might imagine themselves as beneath the empires who claimed their lands, but not as part of them, not subsumed in the colonial context and the rules that colonizers proposed for arranging the Chamorro identity.

The Chamorro existed, but as a local, minor subject. This subject was capable of weaving, fishing, farming, singing, laughing, crying and praying, but was always trapped within the particular, never able to shoulder the position of universality, meaning able to have a consciousness that could be considered national, international, global.[78] The Chamorro could be colorful and beautiful on a small scale only, always stuck to a small island and only capable of representing his or her own tragic, shattered existence. This subjectivity was sustained through ideologies of durability, endurance and survival, but not vitality or agency. The Chamorro was equated with the weathered nature of latte stones, but not with the ability to construct and build great things. The Chamorro subject became associated with whispers of the past, but not possibilities for the future.

---

76   Rogers, 104.
77   See Chapter 2, Bevacqua, *These May or May Not*, Chapter 2.
78   Denise Da Silva, *Towards a Global Idea of Race* (Minneapolis: University of Minnesota Press, 2007).

This is not a version of sovereignty unique to Chamorros, but rather an affliction that many colonized peoples face. They are marked as passive parts of history, not active ones. They end up accepting the idea that they needed to be civilized, discovered or liberated by others in order to exist. As a result, they will generally downplay their own role in history and instead elevate those who seem more powerful and more capable. Their own powerful and important roles in history may end up being lost or forgotten as well.

MANOT'FULU'HACHA: Heroic Impossibility

Confronted with the story of the Uprising at Atåte and the Men of Malesso' who liberated themselves, Chamorros found that it stood in contrast to so many things they had come to believe about themselves and the ways in which they had experienced the war. Whereas the brave but passive *"minesngon"* experiences of most Chamorros fit quite comfortably within a paradigm where U.S. liberation was at the apex and every manner of Chamorro resistance was dependent upon a U.S. return, the Uprising at Atåte complicated this. The experiences of most Chamorros fit within the colonial binary, where their experiences were small and those of the United States and its soldiers were large, but the Men of Malesso' acted at Atåte in ways that would easily resist such diminutive symbolization. When those men defeated their militarized imperial hegemonic Japanese colonizers, they won a place not beneath the United States, but beside them as liberators of the island and the Chamorro people.

The Uprising at Atåte was not motivated by patriotism or loyalty to the United States, but rather as an act of self-preservation and a defense of family in the face of almost certain annihilation. While many acts that Chamorros undertook during *I Tiempon Chapones* and other periods were not necessarily performed in the name of the

United States, they could still be subsumed within an overpowering narrative of U.S. patriotism and liberation. Atåte cannot.

In contemporary commemorative narratives of Tinta and Fåha, Chamorros suffer and endure. Their scars and survival are their rites of passage for their new feelings of devotion to the United States. The United States and a teleology of potential inclusion looms over Tinta and Fåha. Atåte is different: the focus is on Chamorros, as they are the actors, the heroes, and because of this, it is a story that is, in its very nature, political. The United States is still part of the story, as the Men of Malesso' paddle out to the U.S. ships seeking aid, acknowledging that their self-liberation may be short-lived without outside help. However, the relationship is clearly different.

The Uprising at Atåte challenges the idea of the United States as the sole liberator of the island and Chamorros as just passive beneficiaries. Atåte insists that a group of Chamorros from Malesso' share the same honors as the venerated U.S. military. Atåte disrupts the idea that Chamorros are purely passive and require someone else to fight for them, and Atåte shows that Chamorros have the potential to protect themselves and to take charge over their destiny.

The Uprising at Atåte was an event that Chamorros after *I Tiempon Chapones* could not integrate into their self-conceptualization, and also it did not seem to fit into the way the canonical Chamorro narrative was being formed under the resurgent U.S. imperial colonizer. Atåte is regularly discussed, but, as I said earlier in this essay, it is almost always shorn of its more meaningful components, and is sometimes reduced to a scrap of trivia.

The first post-*Tiempon Chapones* Guam history text reflects this neutralizing impulse. Written by Remedios Perez in 1946 for use in the public school system, the text is by no means comprehensive, but simply an overview of important Guam events and dates. It includes a section on *I Tiempon Chapones*, even though this period had just ended a year prior. In that section, there is no mention of Atåte, whereas the brutal slaughter of Chamorros at Tinta and Fåha is highlighted as significant and worthy of children's attention in learning their history. However, a courageous act of Chamorros rising up to protect themselves and their own families and village was somehow not.[79] This would become the standard canonical story following *I Tiempon Chapones*.

MANOT'FULU'HUGUA: *Tayuyute' Ham*[80]

Robert Underwood's article "Red, Whitewash and Blue" begins in Malesso' with a particular monument there known as the *Tayayute' Ham* Memorial erected in the early 1950s by the people of Malesso' to commemorate their collective trauma and memory from the war. The *Tayayute' Ham* Memorial lists the names of those who were killed and those who survived in the massacres at Tinta and Fåha. It makes no reference to the Uprising at Atåte or to the Men of Malesso' who responded to the earlier massacres by killing the Japanese in the village.

Underwood touts the memorial as radical because of the way it defied what was becoming the norm under the return of U.S. rule after *I Tiempon Chapones*, namely to celebrate the United States. For Underwood, the memorial appears to be a Chamorro-focused act of commemoration. Unlike other monuments that were directly tied to honoring the United States or formed in a patriotic context, this monument makes no mention of the United States but focuses on a Catholic community memorial for Chamorro people who suffered and died. The memorial is even more impressive to Underwood as it

---

79 Remedios Perez, *Guam: Past and Present* (Hagåtña, Guam: Department of Education, 1948), 121.

80 *Translation*: Pray for us.

is written in the Chamorro language.⁸¹ The *Tayayute' Ham* Memorial found a way of commemorating the war, remembering those who suffered, and those who survived, without any mention of the United States.

This memorial is a testament to the passively sovereign Chamorro. The failure to include the Uprising at Atåte and the Men of Malesso' in this memorial or even to provide a separate memorial for Atåte is tied to the general lack of appropriate native nationalist symbolism for Chamorros. This lack is not due to the village only, but is part of the collective Chamorro imagination and its limits. The people did not see any political dimension to the Uprising at Atåte. Atåte broke too much from the common Chamorro self-conceptions and the newly forming common narrative they would use to imagine themselves in grateful and submissive relation to the United States.

MANOT'FULU'TULU: *Finakpo'*⁸²

Chamorro identity has shifted significantly since *I Tiempon Chapones*. Where once the term "Chamorro nationalist" would have seemed impossible, today it can be invoked regularly in both positive and negative ways. At the discursive level, Chamorros have come to articulate again a potential politically sovereign aspect to themselves, whether as the basis for their rights as a native people or their aspirations for an independent or decolonized future.

This has led to increased consciousness amongst Chamorros with regards to issues of their culture and identity and how these forces are shaped by their history and the types of narratives that come to give it meaning. Critical scholars since World War II have taken on

---

81 Underwood, "Red, Whitewash," 6.
82 *Translation:* End, Ending.

the task of trying to decolonize much of Chamorro history and find those stories of Chamorro sovereignty, agency and vitality that are usually sacrificed in order to create colonial narratives. Much of the current changes in Chamorro consciousness are tied to becoming more accustomed to a past that once signified tragedy and power of our colonizers but now signifies events of power and resistance to oppression, such as the Uprising at Atåte that allow us to perceive our journey to the present in a completely new manner.

The dominant representations of Chamorro actions during *I Tiempon Chapones*, and other colonial interpretations of Chamorro history can seem to limit future possibilities for Chamorros. Chamorros can easily conceive of themselves as subjects whose only grandeur is stolen grandeur, whose past is only great because of those who have brought greatness to Guam through their travels, their wars, their desires, their interests and their actions. In terms of finding agency that they can call their own, something essential in terms of imagining future possibility, their history is a wasteland of time, in which they play background characters or minor supporting roles. Their only real form of agency is to hitch their destiny to someone larger than themselves and then simply enjoy the ride.

The Uprising at Atåte is an important reminder, even amidst a deluge of accounts of Chamorro dependency, devotion and newborn patriotism during *I Tiempon Chapones*, that the Chamorro has always existed and continues to exist as something more than what its colonizer can account for. Those dominant representations run the risk of obscuring or minimizing the Chamorro elements of their own history and making it so that a story that should inspire and be celebrated is forgotten or becomes unintelligible. Chamorros have existed as a people for thousands of years. The relationship to the United States represents a small but obviously very recent and contemporary portion of that continuum of existence. If we allow the history of Chamorros to be subsumed in this manner, we also create the conditions where their future will take on the same dependent, colonized character. To revisit our history, to restudy it and rearticulate it and draw out events such as Atåte can create Chamorro narratives that are empowering and rich with political possibility.

Michael Lujan Bevacqua, Ph.D., is the curator of the Guam Museum and a former Assistant Professor of Chamorro Studies in the College of Liberal Arts and Social Sciences at the University of Guam.

APPENDICES

APPENDIX 1

List of Chamorros Massacred at Tinta on July 19, 1944

Acfalle, Fausto Chargualaf [1]

Acfalle, Vicente Reyes [2]

Aguigui, Felix Tyquiengco [2]

Babauta, Juan Cruz

Baza, Maria Baza

Baza, Rosa Taijeron

Champaco, Vicente Acfalle [2]

Charfauros, Arthur Benedict Lujan [2]

Cruz, Ramon Padilla [1]

Garrido, Ramon Garrido

Leon Guerrero, Jesus Castro

Lujan, Juan Espinosa

Manalisay, Prudencio Acfalle

Meno, Jose Meno [2]

Mesa, Maria Lukban

Quidagua, Pedro Charguane

APPENDIX 2

Survivors of the Tinta Massacre

Acfalle, Jose Babauta

Anderson, Francisco G.[2]

Anderson, Jesus Cruz[2]

Barcinas, Joaquin Cruz[2]

Charfauros, Manuel Taitano[1]

Concepcion, Joaquina E.

Cruz, Felipe Santiago[2]

Cruz, Tomas Espinosa[1]

Garrido, Ramon E.

Leon Guerrero, Jose Garrido

San Nicolas, Juan C.

Santos, Luisa Baza

Soriano, Ignacio Meno

Tajalle, Tomas Tajalle[2]

[1]Father of a U.S. Navyman

[2]U.S. Navyman

APPENDIX 3

List of Chamorros Massacred at Fåha July 16, 1944

Acfalle, Juan Champaco

Acfalle, Miguel Manalisay

Aguon, Pedro Chargualaf

Barcinas, Jose Tyquiengco

Champaco, Jose Eguiguan

Chargualaf, Cresencio Meno

Cruz, Antonio Cruz

Cruz, Cristobal Leon Guerrero

Cruz, Joaquin Reyes

Cruz, Jose Cruz

Espinosa, Jose Tyquiengco

Fegurgur, Antonio Champaco

Garrido, Ignacio Chargualaf

Garrido, Tomas Sablan

Garrido, Vicente Chargualaf

Guzman, Juan Concepcion

Manibusan, Jose Manibusan

Mansapit, Jesus Maguadog

Mansapit, Santiago Naputi

Mata, Vicente Manalisay

Meno, Dometro Quinene

Meno, Felipe Meno

Meno, Pedro Chargualaf

Quidagua, Jose Charguane

Quidagua, Vicente Charguane

Quinene, Vicente Reyes

Taijeron, Antonio Soriano

Taijeron, Juan Soriano

Topasna, Juan Inocencio

Tyquiengco, Franciso Babauta

APPENDIX 4

Log of the U.S.S. Wadsworth, DD-516, July 22, 1944

A day after the Japanese were massacred at Atâte, six volunteers were picked up by the U.S.S. *Wadsworth* and their names were recorded in the following image of the ship's log for July 22, 1944.

PART II
CONFIDENTIAL

Page 317

UNITED STATES SHIP **WADSWORTH (DD516)** Saturday 22 July 1944

Zone description **-10**

OPERATIONAL AND
ADMINISTRATIVE REMARKS

Position	0800	1200	2000
Lat.	13° 15' N.	13° 26' N.	13° 10' N.
Long.	144° 39' E.	144° 35' E.	144° 04.5' E.

00-04

Steaming in station #7(7090), of A/S screen for T.G. 53.2, in cruising disposition 3T, on base course 275° T&G 277° PSC, at fleet speed 12.5 knots. Guide and OTC in GEORGE CLYMER. Ship darkened in material condition "BAKER", condition of readiness II MIKE. Boilers #2 and #4 on main line. 0005 changed base course and axis to 225° T&G 238° PSC. 0025 changed base course and axis to 180° T&G 185° PSC. 0045 changed base course and axis to 135° T&G 134° PSC. 0105 changed base course and axis to 083° T&G 071° PSC.

A.L. ROTH, Lieutenant (jg), U.S.N.R.

04-08

Steaming as before. 0530 sighted GUAM bearing 083° T., distance 17 miles. 0641 changed fleet course and axis to 090° T&G 080° PSC. 0653 changed fleet speed to 8 knots. 0715 proceeding to patrol station #11 of GUAM screen. 0745 on patrol station #11, patrolling on line of bearing 112° T. - 292° T., distance 7,500 yards, near southern end of GUAM. 0746 men sighted bearing 112° T., in boat. 0758 took aboard 6 CHAMORRO natives, named as follows: CRUZ, Juan A.; GARRIDO, Juan M.; MANALISAY, Joaquin C.; TORRES, Jose M.; Cruz, Antonio L.G.; BARRINAS, Jesus C.;

N.B. HOLT, Lieutenant, U.S.N.R.

08-12

Steaming as before. 0815 mustered crew on stations, no absentees. 0817 on various courses at various speeds proceeding to U.S.S. GEORGE CLYMER. 0852 the following men were transferred to the U.S.S. GEORGE CLYMER: Jesus C. BARRINAS; Antonio L.G. CRUZ; Jose M. TORRES; Joaquin C. MANALISAY; Juan M. GARRIDO; and Juan M. CRUZ. 0854 proceeding to patrol station #23 on various courses at various speeds. 0903 made daily inspection of magazines and smokeless powder samples, conditions normal. 1000 commenced patrolling station #23 on line of patrol 0000° - 180° T., at 10 knots. Limits of patrol OROTE POINT, bearing 071° T., and south tangent of GUAM, bearing 127° T. 1112 at various speeds proceeding to station #16. 1128 commenced patrolling station #16, on line of patrol 075° - 235° T., distance of patrol 3.5 miles. Northern limit 1 mile off of OROTE POINT.

A.L. ROTH, Lieutenant (jg), U.S.N.R.

12-16

Steaming as before.

R.M. FISHER, Lieutenant (jg), U.S.N.R.

16-18

Steaming as before. 1603 passed mail to ANTHONY. 1605 stood back into patrol area and commenced patrol at 10 knots. 1737 commenced forming cruising disposition 3-T, on fleet course and axis 230° T&G 232° PSC, speed 8 knots.

Approved:
WALSH, Commander, U.S.N.
Commanding Officer.

Examined:
HAGERMAN, Lieutenant, U.S.N.
Navigator.

To be forwarded direct to the Bureau of Naval Personnel at the end of each month.

APPENDIX 4

Log of the U.S.S. George S. Clymer APA-27
July 22, 29-30, 1944

The following images are from the ship's log for the U.S.S. *George Clymer* from July 22, 29 and 30, 1944. It mentions the first group of six volunteers who paddled for help after the massacre at Atåte, as well as a second group that followed a week later.

PART III
CONFIDENTIAL

Page 204

UNITED STATES SHIP GEORGE CLYMER (APA27) Saturday 22 July, 1944

Zone description -10

Position	0800	1200	2000
Lat.		13°-24'N	
Long.		144°-35'E	

OPERATIONAL REMARKS
(WAR DIARY)

0-4 Steaming as before on course 270°(t), 271°(pgc), 270°(psc), at 12.5 knots, 58 rpm in company with designated ships of T.G. 53.2 in cruising formation 3-T. CLYMER, flagship of C.T.G. 53.2, formation guide. 0005 Changed course to 225°(t), 226°(pgc), 227°(psc). 0025 Changed course to 180°(t), 181°(pgc), 191°(psc). 0045 Changed course to 135°(t), 136°(pgc), 142°(psc). 0105 Changed course to 083°(t), 083°(pgc), 084°(psc).

R. B. MC COLLUM, Lieut., D-V(S), USNR.

4-8 0504 Exercised at general quarters. 0556 Changed standard speed to 14 knots, 69 rpm. 0604 Secured from general quarters, set condition III(M). 0641 Changed course to 090°(t), 091°(pgc), 087°(psc). 0652 Steaming on various courses and at various speeds approaching transport area, Agat Bay, Guam.

R. SCARRITT, Jr., Lt.(jg), D-V(G), USNR.

8-12 0810 Commenced discharging cargo. 0855 Received the following natives of Guam aboard: Jose Tones, Juan A. Cruz, Joaquin M. Maualisay, Antouis L. Zecruz, Juan M. Garido, Jesus C. Barsunas.

C. ECCLESTON, Lieut., D-V(G), USNR.

12-16 1410 Received LST 446 alongside to port. 1415 Received LCT 966 alongside to starboard. 1526 LST 446 cast off. 1555 Received LST 482 alongside to port. 1556 The following natives of Guam came aboard: Felipe S. Cruz, Jesus A. Cruz, Jesus A. Cruz, Joaquin C. Barunas, Jesus C. Castro, Tomas T. Tajalle.

J. R. TRACEY, Lt.(jg), D-V(G), USNR.

16-20 1815 LST 482 cast off. 1610 Captain Adolph E. BECKER, Jr., USN, ComGenIstProvBaseHq and staff reported aboard for transportation.

J. R. TRACEY, Lt.(jg), D-V(G), USNR.

20-24 No remarks.

L. Q. PATTON, Lieut., D-V(S), USNR.

Approved:
_____ Captain, U. S. Navy.
Commanding Officer.

Examined:
C. ECCLESTON, Lieut., D-V(G), USNR.
Navigator.

To be forwarded direct to the Commander in Chief, U. S. Fleet, either at end of an operation or at the end of the calendar month.

NAVPERS 126

NAVPERS 126

DECLASSIFIED
Authority NND 927405
NND 803052

PART III
CONFIDENTIAL

Page 211

UNITED STATES SHIP GEORGE CLYMER (APA27)	Saturday (Day)	29 (Date)	July (Month)	1944

Zone description -10

Position	0800	1200	2000
Lat.		13°-23'N	
Long.		144°-37'E	

OPERATIONAL REMARKS
(WAR DIARY)

0-4 Lying to in the transport area, Agat Bay, Guam Island. Flagship of CTG 53.2.

R. B. MC COLLUM, Lieut., D-V(S), USNR.

4-8 0505 Exercised at general quarters. 0605 Secured from general quarters, set condition III(N)

W. S. MOREY, Lieut., D-V(G), USNR.

8-12 1100 While coming alongside this vessel in LCM, YUARRA, Fanatino Lopez, S2c, Boat Pool #16, left foot was caught between LCM and ship, caused by swell, Diagnosis: amputation of left foot proximal to the four toes and a portion of the great toe.

R. S. RUNYAN, Lieut., D-V(G), USNR.

12-16 1330 Pursuant to orders of ComGr4PhibsPac, Lieut. R. F. DUPUY, A-V(S), USNR, was detached from duty with ComGr4PhibsPac to proceed and carry out basic orders.

R. K. KENDALL, Lt.(jg), D-V(G), USNR.

16-20 1910 The following natives of Guam were transferred aboard for questioning: Pedro Q. Sanchez, Juan M. Aguan, Ziers Hire.

P. A. MC KINNEY, Ens., D-V(G), USNR.

20-24 No remarks.

R. SCARRITT, jr., Lt.(jg), D-V(G), USNR.

Approved:
_____ Captain, U. S. Navy,
Commanding Officer.

Examined:
C. ECCLESTON, Lieut., D-V(G), USNR.
Navigator.

DECLASSIFIED
Authority NND 927605
NND 803052

PART III
CONFIDENTIAL

Page 212

UNITED STATES SHIP GEORGE CLYMER (APA27)	Sunday	30	July	1944
	(Day)	(Date)	(Month)	

Zone description -10

Position	0800	1200	2000
Lat.		13°-23'N	
Long.		144°-39'E	

OPERATIONAL REMARKS
(WAR DIARY)

0-4 Lying to in transport area, Agat Bay, Guam Island. Flagship of CTG 53.2.

W. S. Morey
W. S. MOREY, Lieut., D-V(G), USNR.

4-8 0505 Exercised at general quarters. 0605 Secured from general quarters, set condition III(M)

R. B. McCollum
R. B. MC COLLUM, Lieut., D-V(S), USNR.

8-12 0930 The following named natives of Guam Island left the ship and returned to Guam Island:
Pedro Q. Sanchez, Juan M. Aguan, Ziers Rio.

R. K. Kendall
R. K. KENDALL, Lt.(jg), D-V(G), USNR.

12-16 No remarks.

P. A. McKinney
P. A. MC KINNEY, Ens., D-V(G), USNR.

16-20 No remarks.

H. S. Runyan
H. S. RUNYAN, Lieut., D-V(G), USNR.

20-24 No remarks.

W. S. Morey
W. S. MOREY, Lieut., D-V(G), USNR.

Approved: _____ Captain, U. S. Navy.
Commanding Officer.

Examined: *C. Eccleston*
C. ECCLESTON, Lieut., D-V(G), USNR.
Navigator.

To be forwarded direct to the Commander in Chief, U. S. Fleet, either at end of an operation or at the end of the calendar month.

APPENDIX 5

Fåha Massacre Memorial Sites

The following images are memorials created by the people of Malesso' in remembrance of the victims of the massacre at Fåha. Photographs by Robert Tenorio. Courtesy of Jose M. Torres.

APPENDIX 6

Tinta Massacre Memorials

The following images are memorials created by the people of Malesso', in remembrance of the victims and survivors of the massacre at Tinta. Photographs by Robert Tenorio. Courtesy of Jose M. Torres.

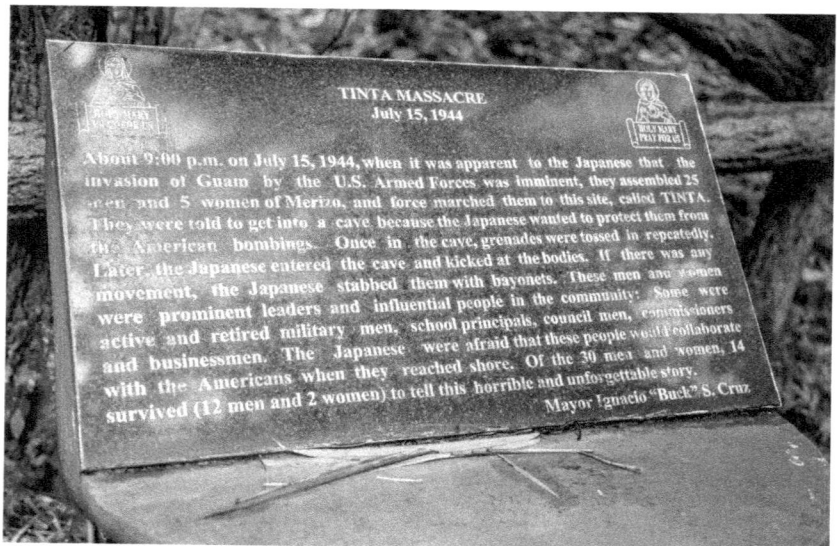

www.ingramcontent.com/pod-product-compliance
Lightning Source LLC
Chambersburg PA
CBHW061808070526
44586CB00024B/2757